THE

UPRISING OF A GREAT PEOPLE.

THE UNITED STATES IN 1861.

TO WHICH IS ADDED

A WORD OF PEACE

ON THE DIFFERENCE BETWEEN ENGLAND AND THE UNITED STATES.

FROM THE FRENCH OF

COUNT AGÉNOR DE GASPARIN.

BY MARY L. BOOTH.

NEW AMERICAN EDITION,
FROM THE AUTHOR'S REVISED EDITION.

NEW YORK:
CHARLES SCRIBNER, 124 GRAND STREET.
1862.

JOHN F. TROW,
PRINTER, STEREOTYPER, AND ELECTROTYPER,
46, 48 & 50 Greene Street,
New York.

TRANSLATOR'S PREFACE

TO THE REVISED AMERICAN EDITION.

THE edition of the *Uprising of a Great People* which we issue herewith, has been carefully revised to conform to the new edition of the original work, just published at Paris. The author has corrected several errors of fact, which were noted by American reviewers on the appearance of the translation, and has also made sundry changes in the work, designed to bring it down to the present time, and to adapt its counsels to the new light that is breaking in upon us in the progress of events. These changes, however, have been few, and relate chiefly to the policy of emancipation, for so truly has this remarkable book proved a prophecy, that the author, on reviewing it after a lapse of several eventful months, can find nothing to strike out as having proved untrue. We are indebted to the kindness of Count de Gasparin for one or two corrections of trifling biographical misstatements in the translator's preface.

The pamphlet concerning the Trent affair, and the surrender of Messrs. Mason and Slidell, which we append to this edition, will be read with interest at the present crisis, as an able exposition of the views of European statesmen on the international difficulty which has sprung so unexpectedly upon us. While it justifies the surrender on the ground of technical error, it utters a solemn warning in the name of Europe, that, if the demand were a mere pretext to force us into a ruinous war, such a proceeding will not again be tolerated. This pamphlet, entitled *Une Parole de Paix*, is the article which appeared in the *Journal des Débats*, December 11, 12, and 13, since published as a *brochure*, with some additions.

This new edition is especially valuable, inasmuch as it seals the faith of our noble friend and sympathizer. "A few months ago," says Count de Gasparin, in his preface, "I believed in the uprising of a great people; now I am sure of it." Let not the issue shame us by disappointing his trust!

MARY L. BOOTH.

NEW YORK, *February*, 1862.

PREFACE

TO THE SECOND EDITION.

I HAVE nothing to change in these pages. When I wrote them before the breaking out of the American crisis, I foreboded, which was not difficult, that the crisis would be long and grievous, that there would be mistakes and reverses; but I foreboded, also, that through these mistakes and reverses, an immense progress was about to come to light. Some have undertaken to doubt it: at the sight of civil war, and the evils which it necessarily entails, at the recital of one or two defeats, they have hastened to raise their hands to Heaven, and to proclaim in every key the ruin of the United States.

This is not the place to discuss judgments, sometimes superficial, sometimes malevolent, which too often pass current among us; to examine what has been, what should be the attitude of our Europe, what is our responsibility, what are our interests and our duties. We alone, I am ashamed to admit it, we alone run the risk of rendering doubtful the final triumph of the good cause;

we have not ceased to be, in spite of ourselves, the only chance and the only hope of the champions of slavery.

Perhaps I shall enter ere long, in a new study, upon the important subject which I confine myself to indicating here, and which pre-occupies the government at Washington to such a degree that it seems inclined to order defensive preparations in view of an unnatural conflict between liberal America and ourselves. Every thing may happen—alas! the seemingly impossible like all else. It is not enough, therefore, to declare this impossible and monstrous, it is not enough to prove that the present state of feeling in Europe is far from giving reason to foresee an intervention in favor of the South; it is necessary to sap at the base these deplorable sophisms, more fully credited than is imagined, which may, in due time, under the pressure of certain industrial needs or of certain political combinations, urge France and England into a course which is not their own.

For the present, I have only wished to repeat, with a strengthened conviction, what I said a few months ago. I believed then in the uprising of a great people; now I am sure of it.

VALLEYRES, *November* 2, 1861.

TRANSLATOR'S PREFACE.

At this moment, when we are anxiously scrutinizing every indication of European feeling with respect to the American question, the advent of a book, bearing the stamp of a close philosophical, political, and practical study of the subject, and written, withal, in so hopeful a spirit as to make us feel with the writer that whatever may result from the present crisis must be for good, cannot fail to be of public interest and utility. So truly prophetic is this work in its essence, that we can hardly believe that it was written in great part amid the mists that preceded the inauguration of Mr. Lincoln. All probabilities appear to have been foreseen, and the unerring exactness with which events have taken place hitherto precisely in the direction indicated by the author, encourages us to believe that this will continue until his predictions will have been fulfilled to the end. Clear-sighted, philosophical, appreciative of American genius and accomplishment, critical, yet charitable to tenderness, stigmatizing the fault, yet forgiving the offender, cheering our nation onward by words of encouragement, bravely spoken at the needed moment, menacing Europe with the scorn of posterity, if, forgetting her oft-repeated professions, she dare forsake the side of liberty to traffic in principles; such is the scope of what a late reviewer calls " the wisest book which has been written upon America since De Tocqueville."

Few men are better qualified to judge American affairs than Count de Gasparin. A many-sided man, combining the scholar, the statesman, the politician, the man of letters, and the finished gentleman, possessed of every advantage of culture, wealth, and position, he has devoted a long life to the advocacy of liberty in all its forms, whether religious or political, and has ended by making a profound study of American history and politics, the accuracy of which is truly remarkable. A few facts with respect to his career, kindly furnished by his personal friend, Rev. Dr. Robert Baird, of New York, will be here in place.

Count Agénor Étiénne de Gasparin was born at Orange, July 4, 1810. His family is Protestant, and of Corsican origin; his father was a man of talent and position, who served for many years as Prefect of the District of the Rhone, and afterwards as Minister of the Interior under Louis Philippe, by whom he was highly esteemed. He received a liberal education, and devoted himself especially to literature, till 1842, when he was elected by the people of the island of Corsica to represent them in the Chamber of Deputies. Here began his political career. At that time, religious liberty was in danger of perishing in France, assailed by the powerful opposition of the tribunals and the administration. De Gasparin declared himself its champion, and, in an eloquent speech in the Chamber of Deputies, which moved the audience to tears, he boldly accused the courts of perverting the civil code in favor of religious intolerance, and claimed unlimited freedom for evangelical preaching and colportage. He also made strenuous efforts to effect the immediate emancipation of slaves in the French colonies, and published several essays on the subject. He devoted himself especially to the protection of Protestantism, and founded in France the Society for the Protection of Protestant interests, and the Free Protestant Church, yet, detesting religious intolerance everywhere, he did not hesitate to denounce the Protestant persecutions of Sweden as bitterly as he had done the Catholic bigotry of France. He was head of the Cabinet in the Ministry of the Interior while his father was Minister, and was in the Ministry of Public Instruction under M. Guizot. In 1848, while travelling in the East with his wife, a talented Swiss lady, the author of several works, he received intelligence of the downfall of the government of Louis Philippe. This event closed his public career. He addressed a letter of condolence to the dethroned monarch, to whom he was warmly attached, then retired to Switzerland to devote himself to literature and philanthropy, being too warm an adherent of the Orleans dynasty to take part in the new administration. Politically, he is, like Guizot, an advocate of constitutional monarchy. Since the Revolution, he has continued to reside in Switzerland. He has published numerous works on philosophical and social questions, among which may be instanced: *Esclavage et Traite; De l'Affranchissement des Esclaves; Intérêts généraux du Protestantisme Français, Paganism et Christianisme, Des tables tournantes, du surnaturel en général, et des esprits*, etc.

His present work, so hopeful and sympathizing, recommends itself to the attention of the American public; and even those who may dissent from some of his positions or conclusions, cannot but admire his vigorous comprehension of the outlines of the subject, and be cheered by his predictions of the future. As the expression of the opinion of an intelligent, clear-sighted European, in a position to comprehend men and things, concerning the storm which is now agitating the whole country, it can scarcely fail of a hearty welcome. I commend the following interpretation, which I have sought to make as conscientiously literal as due regard to idioms of language would permit, to all true lovers of liberty and of the Union, of whatever State, section, or nation.

MARY L. BOOTH.

NEW YORK, *June* 15, 1861.

PREFACE.

In publishing this study at the present time, I expose myself to the blame of prudent men. I shall be told that I ought to have waited.

To have waited for what? Until there shall be no more great questions in Europe to dispute our attention with the American question? Or until the American question has shaped itself, and we are able to know clearly what interests it will serve, in what consequences it will end?

I am not sorry, I confess, to applaud duty before it is recommended by success. When success shall have come, men eager to celebrate it will not be wanting, and I shall leave to them the care of demonstrating then that the North has been in the right, that it has saved the United States.

To construct the philosophy of events after they have passed is very interesting, without doubt, but the work to be accomplished to-day is far more serious. The point in question is to sustain our friends when they are in need of us; when their battle, far from being won, is scarcely begun; the point in question is to give our support—the very considerable support of European opinion —at the time when it can be of service; the point in question is to assume our small share of responsibility in one of the gravest conflicts of this age.

Let us enlist; for the Slave States, on their part, are losing no time. They have profited well, I must admit, by the advantages assured to them by the complicity of the ministers of Mr. Buchanan. In the face of the inevitable indecision of a new government, around which care had been taken to accumulate in advance every impossibility of acting, the decided bearing of the extreme South, its airs of audacity and defiance have had a certain éclât and a certain success. Already its partisans raise their heads; they dare speak in its favor among us; they insult free trade, by transforming it into an argument destined to serve the interests of slavery. And shall we remain mute? Shall we listen to the counsels of that false wisdom that always comes too late, so much does it fear to declare itself too early? Shall we not feel impelled to show in all its true light the sacred cause of liberty? Ah! I declare that the blood boils in my veins; I have hastened and would gladly have hastened still more. Circumstances independent of my will alone have retarded a publication prepared more than a month ago.

ORANGE, *March* 19, 1861.

CONTENTS.

A GREAT PEOPLE RISING.

INTRODUCTION.

The title of this work will produce the effect of a paradox. The general opinion is that the United States continued to pursue an upward course until the election of Mr. Lincoln, and that since then they have been declining. It is not difficult, and it is very necessary, to show that this opinion is absolutely false. Before the recent victory of the adversaries of slavery, the American Confederation, in spite of its external progress and its apparent prosperity, was suffering from a fearful malady which had well-nigh proved mortal; now, an operation has taken place, the sufferings have increased, the gravity of the situation is revealed for the first time, perhaps, to inattentive eyes. Does this mean that the situation was not grave when it did not appear so? Does this mean that we must deplore a violent crisis which alone can bring the cure?

1*

I do not deplore it—I admire it. I recognize in this energetic reaction against the disease, the moral vigor of a people habituated to the laborious struggles of liberty. The rising of a people is one of the rarest and most marvellous prodigies presented by the annals of humanity. Ordinarily, nations that begin to decline, decline constantly more and more; a rare power of life is needed to retrieve their position, and stop in its course a decay once begun.

We have a strange way of seconding the generous enterprise into which the United States have entered with so much courage! We prophesy to them nothing but misfortunes; we almost tell them that they have ceased to exist; we give them to understand, that in electing Mr. Lincoln they have renounced their greatness; that they have precipitated themselves head foremost into an abyss; that they have ruined their prosperity, sacrificed their future, rendered henceforth impossible the magnificent character which was reserved to them. Mr. Buchanan, we seem to say, is the last President of the Union.

This, thank God, is the reverse of the truth. But lately, indeed, the United States were advancing to their ruin; but lately there was reason to mourn in thinking of them; the steps might have been counted which it remained for them to take to complete the union of their destiny with that of an accursed and perishable institution—an institution which corrupts and destroys every thing with which it comes in contact. To-day, new prospects are opening to them; they will have to combat, to labor, to suffer; the crime of a century is not repaired in a day; the right path when long forsaken is not found again without effort; guilty traditions and old complicities are not broken through without sacrifices. It is none the less true, notwithstanding, that the hour of effort and of sacrifice, grievous as it may be, is the very hour of deliverance. The election of Mr. Lincoln will be one of the great dates of American history; it closes the past, but it opens the future. With it is about to commence, if the same spirit be maintained, and if excessive concessions do not succeed in undoing all that has been done, a new era, at once purer and greater than that which has just ended.

Let others accuse me of optimism; I willingly agree to it. I believe that optimism is often right here below. We need hope; we need sometimes to receive good news; we need to see sometimes the bright side of things. The bright side is often the true side; if Love is blindfolded, I see a triple bandage on the eyes of Hate. Kindliness has its privileges; and I do not think myself in a worse position than another to judge the United States because they inspire me with an earnest sympathy; because, after having mourned their faults and trembled at their perils, I have joyfully saluted the noble and manly policy of which the election of Mr. Lincoln is the symptom. Is it not true, that at the first news we all seemed to breathe a whiff of pure and free air from the other side of the ocean?

It is a pleasure, in times like ours, to feel that certain principles still live; that they will be obeyed, cost what it may; that questions of conscience can yet sometimes weigh down questions of profit. The abolition of slavery will be, I have always thought, the principal conquest of the nineteenth century. This will be its recommendation in the eyes of posterity, and the chief compensation for many of its weaknesses. As for us old soldiers of emancipation, who have not ceased to combat for it for twenty years and more, at the tribunal and elsewhere, we shall be excused without doubt for seeing in the triumph of our American friends something else than a subject of lamentation.

CHAPTER I.

AMERICAN SLAVERY.

If they had not triumphed, do you know who would have gained the victory? Slavery is only a word—a vile word, doubtless, but to which we in time become habituated. To what do we not become habituated? We have stores of indulgence and indifference for the social iniquities which have found their way into the current of cotemporary civilization, and which can invoke prescription. So we have come to speak of American slavery with perfect sang froid. We are not, therefore, to stop at the word, but to go straight to the thing; and the thing is this:

Every day, in all the Southern States, families are sold at retail: the father to one, the mother to another, the son to a third, the young daughter to a fourth; and the father, the mother, the children, are scattered to the four winds of heaven; these hearts are broken, these poor beings are given a prey to infamy and sorrow, these marriages are ruptured, and adulterous unions are formed twenty leagues, a hundred leagues away, in the bosom and with the assent of a Christian community. Every day, too, the domestic slave-trade carries on its work; merchants in human flesh ascend the Mississippi, to seek in the *producing* States wherewith to fill up the vacuum caused unceasingly by slavery in the *consuming* States; their ascent made, they scour the farms of Virginia or of Kentucky, buying here a boy, there a girl; and other hearts are torn, other families are dispersed, other nameless crimes are accomplished coolly, simply, legally: it is the necessary revenue of the one, it is the indispensable supply of the others. Must not the South live, and how dares any one travesty a fact so simple? by what right was penned that eloquent calumny called "Uncle Tom's Cabin"?

A calumny! I ask how any one would set to work to calumniate the customs which I have just described. Say, then, that the laws of the South are a calumny, that the official acts of the South are a calumny; for I affirm that the simple reading of these acts and these laws, a glance at the advertisements of a Southern journal, saddens the heart more, and wounds the conscience deeper, than the most poignant pages of Mrs. Harriet Beecher Stowe. I admit willingly that there are many masters who are very kind and very good. I admit that there are some slaves who are relatively happy. I cast aside unhesitatingly the stories of exceptional cruelty; it is enough for me to see that these *happy* slaves expose themselves to a thousand deaths to escape a situation declared "preferable to that of our workmen." It is enough for me to hear the heart-rending cries of those women and young girls who, adjudged to the highest and last bidder, become, by the law and in a Christian country, the property, yes, the property (excuse the word, it is the true one) of the debauchees, their purchasers. And remark here that the virtues of the master are a weak guarantee: he may die, he may become bankrupt, and nothing then can hinder his slaves from being sold into the hands of the buyer who scours the country and makes his choice.

We should calumniate the South if we amused ourselves by making a collection of atrocious deeds, in the same manner that we should calumniate France by seeking in the *Police Gazette* for the description of her social state. There is, notwithstanding, this difference between the iniquities of slavery and our own: the first are almost always unpunished, while the second are repressed by the courts. An institution which permits evil, creates it in a great measure: in saying that men are things, it necessarily engenders more crimes, more acts of violence, more cowardly deeds, than the imagination of romancers will ever invent. When a class has neither the right to complain, nor to defend itself, nor to testify in law; when it cannot make its voice heard in any manner, we may be excused for not taking in earnest the idyls chanted on its felicity. We must be ignorant at once of the heart of man and of history to preserve the slightest doubt on this point. I add that those who, like me, have had in their hands the documents of our colonial slavery, have become terribly suspicious, and are likely to look with a skeptical eye on these Arcadian descriptions, the worth of which they can appreciate.

Once more, I do not contest the humanity of many masters, but I remember that there were humane masters too in Martinique, Guadeloupe, and Bourbon; yet this did not prevent the discovery, on a rigid scrutiny, sometimes of excesses, as fearful as inevitable, of the discretionary power; at others, of a systematic depravation, and this to such a point that in one of our colonies the custom of regular unions had become absolutely unknown to the slaves.

I cannot help believing that man is the same everywhere. Never, in any time or in any latitude, has it been given him to possess his fellow, without fearful misfortunes having resulted to both. Have we not heard celebrated the delightful mildness of Spanish slavery in Cuba? Travellers entertained by the Creoles usually return enchanted with it. Yet, notwithstanding, it is found that on quitting the cities and penetrating into the plantations, the most barbarous system of labor is discovered that exists in the entire world. Cuba devours her black population so rapidly that she is unceasingly obliged to purchase negroes from abroad; and these, being once on the island, have not before them an average life exceeding ten years! In the United States, the planters of the extreme South are also obliged to renew their supply of negroes; but, as they have recourse to the domestic instead of the African trade, and as the domestic trade furnishes slaves at an excessively high price, it follows that motives of interest oppose the adoption of the destructive system of Cuba. Other higher motives also oppose it, I am certain; and I am far from comparing the system of Louisiana or the Carolinas to that which prevails in the Spanish island. We exaggerate nothing, however; and whatever may be the points of difference, we may hold it as certain that those of resemblance are still more numerous: the tree is the same, it cannot but bear the same fruits.

It must be affirmed, besides, that slavery is peculiarly odious on that soil where the equality of mankind has been inscribed with so much eclat at the head of a celebrated constitution. Liberty imposes obligations; there is at the bottom of the human conscience something which will always cause slavery to be more scandalous at Washington than at Havana. What happens in the United States will be denounced more violently, more loudly, than what happens in Brazil; and this is right.

This said, I pause: I have not the slightest wish to introduce here a perfectly superfluous discussion on the principle and the consequences of slavery. I know all with which Americans reproach us Europeans. It was we, Frenchmen, Englishmen, Spaniards, Hollanders, who imposed on them this institution which we take delight in combating—this inheritance which we anathematize! Before attacking slavery, we would do well to turn our attention to our own crimes—to the oppression of the weak in our manufactories, for instance! But these retaliatory arguments have the fault of proving nothing at all. We will leave them; we have said enough on the nature of American slavery; let us proceed to the special subject of our work.

CHAPTER II.

WHERE THE UNITED STATES WERE DRIFTING BEFORE THE ELECTION OF MR. LINCOLN.

I HAVE spoken of the great perils which the United States encountered before the election of Mr. Lincoln. The time has come to enter into some details in justification of this proposition, which must have appeared strange at first sight, but the terms of which I have weighed well: if the slavery party had again achieved a victory, the United States would have gone to ruin. Here are the facts:

Formerly, there was but one opinion among Americans on the subject of slavery. The Southerners may have considered it as a necessary evil; in any case, they considered it as an evil. Carolina herself nobly resisted its introduction upon her soil; other colonies did the same. Washington inscribed the wish in his will that so baleful an institution might be promptly suppressed. To pen up slavery, to prevent its extension, to reduce it to the *rôle* of a local and temporary fact, which it was determined to restrain still more—such was the sentiment which prevailed in the South, as in the North. And, in fact, slavery was ere long abolished in the majority of the States composing the Union. To-day, slavery has become a beneficent, evangelical institution, the corner-stone of republics, the foundation of all liberties; it has become a source of blessings for the blacks as for the whites. We not only are not to think of reducing the number of slave States, but it becomes important to increase them unceasingly: to interdict to slavery the entrance into a new territory is almost iniquitous. Such are the theories proclaimed by the governors, by the legislators of the cotton States; they propose them openly, without scruple and without circumlocution, under the name of political—what do I say? of moral and Christian axioms. For these theories they take fire, they become excited; they feel that enthusiasm which was inspired in other times by the love of liberty. See entire populations, who, under the eye of God, and invoking his support, devote themselves, body, soul, and goods, to the *holy* cause of slavery, its conquests, its indefinite extension, its inter-State and African trade.

And the conquests of slavery do not figure only in platforms; they are pursued and accomplished effectively on the soil of America. In the face of the nineteenth century, free Texas has been transformed into a slave State. To create other slave countries is the aim proposed; and slave countries multiply, and the South does not tolerate the slightest obstacle to conquests of this kind, and it goes forward, and nothing stops it—I am wrong, the election of Mr. Lincoln has stopped it, and this is why its fury breaks out to-day.

One would be furious for less cause! Every thing had gone so well till then! The South spoke as a master, and the North humbly bowed its head before its imperious commands. Its exactions increased from day to day, and it was not difficult to see to what abysses it was leading the entire American Union. Shall we give our readers an idea of this crescendo of pretensions?

We will content ourselves with going back to the last Mexican war and to the Wilmot proviso. This was, as is known, a measure, or *proviso*, stipulating that slavery could not be introduced into conquered provinces. Such was the starting point.

It was sought then, in 1847, to prevent the territorial extension of slavery. This seems to me reasonable enough; and I am not astonished that the Lincoln platform tends simply to return to this primitive policy. The measure passes the House of Representatives, but is defeated in the Senate. Notwithstanding, the American people hold firm to the principle that slavery shall henceforth no longer be extended; it elects, in 1848, the upright Administration of Gen. Taylor. The cause of justice seems about to triumph, when the death of the whig President, succeeded by the feeble Mr. Fillmore, comes to restore good fortune to the Southerners, the *proviso* is forgotten, and the nation, weary of resistance, ends by adopting a series of deplorable compromises.

Beginning from this moment, the progress of the evil is rapid. Among the compromises, the oldest and most respected, dating back to 1820, was that which bore the name of the *Missouri Compromise.* On admitting Missouri as a Slave State, it had been stipulated that slavery should be no longer introduced north of the 36th degree of latitude. Of this limit, so long accepted, the South now complains; it is no longer willing that the development of its "peculiar institution" shall be obstructed in any thing.

Other combats, another victory. A bill proposed by Mr. Douglas annuls the Missouri Compromise, and, based on the principle of local sovereignties, withdraws from Congress the right to interfere in the question of slavery.

The Wilmot proviso could not subsist in the presence of these absolute pretensions. The liberty of slavery (pardon me this mournful and involuntary conjunction) finds an application on the spot. At this juncture, Texas, a province detached from Mexico, is admitted in the quality of a slave State.

What happens then? The partisans of slavery, hampered by nothing any longer, either by limits at the North, or limits at the South, or provisos, or compromises, encounter, to their great horror, an obstacle of quite a different nature. The local sovereignty which they have invoked turns against them; in the Territory of Kansas, the majority votes the exclusion of slavery. At once the Southerners change theory; against local sovereignty they invoke the central power; they demand, they exact that the decisions of the majority in Kansas shall be trodden under foot; they put forward the natural right of slavery. Why shall they be prevented from settling in a Territory with the slaves, their property? When this Territory shall be by and by transformed into a State, there will doubtless be a right to determine the question; but to abolish slavery is quite a different thing from excluding it.

If the South did not win the cause this time, it was not the fault of the government of the United States, but of the inhabitants of Kansas. As for Mr. Buchanan, he showed himself what he has constantly been, the most humble servant of the slavery party. They came together into collision with *squatter sovereignty:* they found for the first time in their path that solid resistance of the West which was manifested in the last election, and which, I firmly hope, is about to save America. But in the mean time, they had taken a new step forward—a formidable step, and one which introduced them into the very bosom of the free States: they had obtained a decision from the Supreme Court—the Dred Scott decree. In the preamble of this too celebrated decision, the highest judicial power of the Confederation did not fear to proclaim two principles: first, that there is no difference between a slave and any other kind of property; secondly, that all American citizens may settle everywhere with their property.

What a menace for the free-soilers! How easy to see to what lengths the South would shortly go! Since slavery constituted property like any other, it was necessary to prohibit the majority from proscribing it in States as well as in Territories. Who knew whether we should not some day see slaves and even slave-markets (the right of property carries with it that of sale) in the streets even of Philadelphia or Boston!

Let no one cry out against this: those who demanded and those who framed the Dred Scott decision knew probably what they wished to do. With the right of property understood in this wise, no State has the power either to vote the real abolition of slavery, or to forbid the introduction of slaves, or to refuse their extradition. And, effectively, horrible laws, ordering fugitive slaves to be given up, were accorded to the violent demands of the South. Liberty by contact with the soil, that great maxim of our Europe, was interdicted America; the very States that most detested slavery were condemned to assist, indignant and shuddering, in the federal invasion of a sheriff entering their homes to lay hands on a poor negro, who had believed in their hospitality, and who was about to be delivered up to the whip of the planter.

It was asking much of the patience of the North; yet, notwithstanding, this patience was not yet at an end. The Administration was given up a prey to the will of the Southerners. On their prohibition, the mails ceased to carry books, journals, letters, which excited their suspicion. They had seized upon the policy of the Union, and they ruled it according to their liking. No one has forgotten those enterprises, favored underhand, then disavowed after failure, those filibustering expeditions in Central America and in the island of Cuba. They were the policy of the South, executed by Mr. Buchanan with his accustomed docility. The point in question was to make conquests, and conquests for slavery. By any means, and at any price, the South was to procure new States. Cuba would furnish some, several would be carved out of Mexico and Central America; for otherwise the slavery majorities would be compromised in Congress, and slavery would be forced to renounce forever the election of the Presidents of free America. To avoid such a misfortune, there is nothing that they would not have been ready to undertake.

Thus, step after step, and exaction after exaction, overthrowing, one after the other, all barriers, the Wilmot proviso, the Missouri Compromise, the right of majorities in the Territories, the very sovereignty of the States annulled by the Dred Scott decision, the South had succeeded in drawing the United States into those violent and dishonest political practices which filled the administration of Mr. Buchanan. The barriers of public probity, and the right of men, yielded in turn; the administration dared write officially that Cuba was necessary to the United States, and that the affranchisement of slaves in Cuba would be a legitimate cause of war. The United States were yoked to the car of slavery: to make slave States, to conquer Territories for slavery, to prevent the terrible misfortune of an abolition of slavery, such was the programme. In negotiations, in elections, nothing else was perceived than this. If the liberty of the seas and the independence of the flag were proudly claimed, it was by the order of the South, and there resulted thence, whether desired or not, a progressive resurrection of the African slave-trade; if candidates in favor of the maintenance of the Union were recommended, it was to assure the conquests of slavery within and without, the invasion of neighboring countries, the extradition of fugitive slaves, the subjugation of majorities rebellious to the South, the suppression of laws disagreeable to the South, the overthrow of the last obstacles which fettered the progress of the South

And it was thus far, to this degree of disorder and abasement, that a noble people had been dragged downwards in the course of years, sinking constantly deeper, abandoning, one by one, its guarantees, losing its titles to the esteem of other nations, approaching the abyss, seeing the hour draw nigh in which to rise would be impossible, bringing down maledictions upon itself, forcing those who love it to reflect on the words of one of its most illustrious leaders: "I tremble for my country, when I remember that God is just!"

All this under the tyrannical and pitiless influence of a minority constantly transformed into a majority! Picture to yourself a man on a vessel standing by the gun-room with a lighted match in his hand; he is alone, but the rest obey him, for at the first disobedience he will blow up himself with all the crew. This is precisely what has been going on in America since she went adrift. The working of the ship was commanded by the man who held the match. "At the first disobedience, we will quit you." Such has always been the language of the Southern States. They were known to be capable of keeping their word; therefore, there ceased to be but one argument in America: secession. "Revoke the compromise, or else secession; modify the legislation of the free States, or else secession; risk adventures, and undertake conquests with us for slavery, or else secession; lastly and above all, never suffer yourselves to elect a president who is not our candidate, or else secession."

Thus spoke the South, and the North submitted. Let us not be unduly surprised at it, there was patriotism in this weakness; many citizens, inimical to slavery, forbore to combat its progress, in order to avoid what appeared to them a greater evil. Declivities like these are descended quickly, and the deplorable presidency of Mr. Buchanan stands to testify to this. The policy of the United States had become doubtful; their good renown was dwindling away even with their warmest friends; their cause was becoming blended more and more with that of servitude; their liberties were compromised, and the Federal institutions were bending before the "institution" of the South; no more rights of the majority before the "institution;" no more sovereignty of the States before the "institution." The ultra policy of Mr. Buchanan had coveted Cuba, essayed violence in Kansas, given up the government of America in fine to a cabinet of such a stamp, that a majority was nearly found in it, ready to disavow Major Anderson, and to order the evacuation of forts of the Confederation, menaced by Carolinian forces.

During this time, an incredible fact had come to light. It was one of the glories of America to have abolished the African slave trade before any other nation, and even to have put it on the same footing with the crime of piracy. The South had openly demanded the re-establishment of a commerce which alone could furinsh it at some day with the number of negroes proportioned to its vast designs. What had Mr. Buchanan done? He doubtless had not consented officially to an enormity which Congress, on its part, would not have tolerated; but repression had become so lax under his administration, that the number of slave ships fitted out in the ports of the United States had at length become very considerable. The port of New York alone, which participates but too much in the misdeeds and tendencies of the South, fitted out eighty-five slavers between the months of February, 1859, and July, 1860. These slavers proudly bore the United States' flag over the seas, and defied the English cruisers. As for the American cruisers, Mr. Buchanan had taken care to remove them all from Cuba, where every one knows that the living cargroes are landed. The slave trade is therefore in the height of prosperity, whatever the last presidential message may say of it, and as to the application of the laws concerning piracy, I do not see that they have had many victims.

We can now measure the perils which menaced the United States. It was not such or such a measure in particular, but a collection of measures, all directed towards the same end, and tending mutually to complete each other: conquests, the domestic and the foreign slave trade, the overthrow of the few barriers opposed to the extension of slavery, the debasement of institutions, the definitive enthroning of an adventurous policy, a policy without principles and without scruples; to this the country was advancing with rapid strides. Do they who raise their hands and eyes to heaven, because the election of Mr. Lincoln has caused the breaking forth of an inevitable crisis, fancy then that the crisis would have been less serious if it had broken forth four years later, when the evil would have been without remedy? Already, the five hundred thousand slaves of the last century have given place to four millions; was it advisable to wait until there were twenty millions, and until vast territories, absorbed by American power, had been peopled by blacks torn from

Africa? Was it advisable to await the time when the South should have become decidedly the most important part of the Confederation, and when the North, forced to secede, should have left to others the name, the prestige, the flag of the United States? Do they fancy that, by chance, with the supremacy of the South, with its conquests, with the monstrous development of its slavery, secession would have been avoided? No! it would have appeared some day as a necessary fact; only it would have been accomplished under different auspices and in different conditions. Such a secession would have been death, a shameful death.

And slavery itself, who imagines, then, that it can be immortal? It is in vain to extend it; it will perish amidst its conquests and through its conquests: one can predict this without being a prophet. But, between the suppression of slavery such as we hope will some time take place, and that which we should have been forced to fear, in case the South had carried it still further, is the distance which separates a hard crisis from a terrible catastrophe. The South knows not what nameless misfortunes it has perhaps just escaped. If it had been so unfortunate as to conquer, if it had been so unfortunate as to carry out its plans, to create slave States, to recruit with negroes from Africa, it would have certainly paved the way, with its own hands, for one of those bloody disasters before which the imagination recoils: it would have shut itself out from all chance of salvation.

It is not possible, in truth, to put an end to certain crimes, and wholly avoid their chastisement; there will always be some suffering in delivering the American Confederation from slavery, and it depends to-day again upon the South to aggravate, in a fearful measure, the pain of the transition. However, what would not have been possible with the election of Mr. Douglas or Mr. Breckenridge, has become possible now with the election of Mr. Lincoln; we are at liberty to hope henceforth for the rising of a great people.

CHAPTER III.

WHAT THE ELECTION OF MR. LINCOLN SIGNIFIES.

I THINK that I have justified the fundamental idea of this work, and the title which I have given it. If the slavery policy had achieved a new triumph; if the North had not elected its President, the first that has belonged to it in full since the existence of the Confederation; if supremacy had not ranged itself in fine on the side with force and justice, this unstable balance would have had its hour of downfall: and what a downfall! Of so much true liberty, of so much progress, of so many noble examples, what would have been left standing? The secession of the South is not the secession of the North; affranchisement with four millions of slaves is not affranchisement with twenty millions; the crisis of 1861 is not that of 1865 or of 1869. The United States, I repeat, with a profound and studied conviction,—the United States have just been saved.

There are those who ask gravely whether the electors of Mr. Lincoln have a plan all ready to effect the abolition of slavery. We answer that this is not in question. Among the influential and earnest men of the victorious party, not one could be cited who would think of proposing any plan whatever of emancipation. One thing alone is proposed: to check the conquests of slavery. That it shall not be extended, that it shall be confined within its present limits, is all that is sought to-day. The policy of the founders of the Confederation has become that of their successors in turn; and to this policy, what can be objected? Is not the sovereignty of the States respected? do they not remain free to regulate what concerns them? do they not preserve the right of postponing, so long as they deem proper, the solution of a dreaded problem? could not this solution be thought over and prepared by those who best know its elements?

The matter is, indeed, more complicated and difficult than is generally imagined. Should we be imprudent enough to meddle with it, we might rightfully be blamed. Here, summary proceedings are evidently not admissible. Time and the spirit of Christianity must do their work by degrees; they will do it, be sure, provided the evil be circumscribed, provided the seat of the conflagration be hemmed in and prevented henceforth from spreading further.

Now, such is the great result acquired by the election of Mr. Lincoln; it is nothing more than this, but it is all this: it is prudence in the present, and it is also the certainty of success in the future. Emancipation is by no means decreed; it will not be for a long time, perhaps: yet the principle of emancipation is established, irrevocably established in the sight of all. Irrevocability has prodigious power over our minds: without being conscious of it, we make way for it; we arrange in view of it our conduct, our plans, and even our doctrines. Once fully convinced that its propagandism is checked, that the future of which it dreamed has no longer any chances of success, the South itself will become accustomed to consider its destiny under a wholly new aspect. The border States, in which emancipation is easy, will range themselves one after another on the side of liberty. Thus the extent of the evil will become reduced of itself, and instead of advancing, as during some years past, towards a colossal development of servitude, it will proceed in the direction of its gradual attenuation.

I reason on the hypothesis of a final maintenance of the Union, whatever may be the incidents of temporary secession. I am not ignorant that there are other hypotheses, which may possibly be realized, and which I shall examine in the course of this treatise; but whatever may happen, I have a full right to call to mind the true scope of the vote which has just been taken. It does not involve the slightest idea of present emancipation; it contents itself with checking the progress of slavery; and to check its progress is, doubtless, to diminish the perils of its future abolition.

It was important to present this observation, for nothing perverts our judgment of the American crisis more than the inexact definitions which are given of abolitionism. We willingly picture abolitionists to ourselves as madmen, seeking to attain their end on the spot, regardless of all else, through blood and ruin! That there may be such is possible, is even inevitable; but the men who exercise any political influence over the North have not for a moment adopted such theories. This is so true, that the other day, at Boston, the people themselves (the people who nominated Mr. Lincoln) dispersed a meeting intended to discuss plans of immediate emancipation.

What if abolitionism, moreover, be a party? what if it make use of the means employed by parties? what if it have its journals, its publicists, its orators? what if it seek allies? what if it be based on interests which may be given it by the majority? what if it appeal to the passions of the North, as the slavery party appeals to those of the South? I do not see, in truth, why this should astonish us. I am far from believing that all the acts of abolitionism are worthy of approbation; I say only that it would be puerile to repudiate a great party for the sole reason that it has the bearing of a party. The duty of citizens in a free country is to choose between parties, and to unite with that whose cause is just and holy. Let them protest against wrong measures, let them refuse to participate in them—nothing can be better; but to withdraw into a sort of political Thebais because the noblest parties have stains on their banner, is, in truth, to turn their back on the civil obligations of real life.

The abolition party is a noble one. Several of its champions have given their lives to propagate their faith. But lately, indeed, the Texan journals took pains to tell us that a number of them had just been hung in that State; and, without even speaking of these noble victims, whose death completes the dishonor of the Southern cause, are there any bolder deeds in the history of mankind than those of the citizens of New England who, to wrest Kansas from slavery, went thither to build their cabins, thus braving a fearful struggle, not only with the slaveholders, but with the President, his illegal measures, and the troops charged with maintaining them?

We must fight to conquer. This seems little understood by those who reproach abolitionism with having been a party militant; to hear them, the true way of bringing about the abolition of slavery was to let it alone: to attack was to exasperate it.

This argument is so unfortunate as to be employed in all bad causes. I remember that when measures were taken against the slave trade, we were told that the sufferings of the slaves would be thus increased, and that the slavers would be *exasperated*. Later, when we held up to the indignation of the whole world the Protestant intolerance of Sweden, we were assured that these public denunciations would put back the question instead of accelerating it. We persevered, and we did rightly. Sweden is advancing, though at too slow a pace, towards religious liberty. It would be difficult to cite any social iniquities that have reformed of themselves; and, since the existence of the world, the method which consists in attacking evil has been the one sanctioned by success. In America itself, the progress made by the border States does not seem to confirm what is told us of the reaction caused by the aggressions of abolitionism. In Virginia, in Kentucky, in Missouri, in Delaware, etc., the liberty party has been continually gaining ground; and the votes received in the slave States by Mr. Lincoln prove it a very great mistake to suppose letting alone to be the condition of progress. Would to God that slavery had not been let alone when the republic of the United States was founded! Then, abolition was easy, the slaves were few in number, and no really formidable antagonism was in play. Unhappily, false prudence made itself heard: it was resolved to keep silence, and not to deprive the South of the honor of a voluntary emancipation—in fine, to reserve the question for the future. The future has bent under the weight of a task which has continued to increase with years, thanks to letting it alone.

A little more letting alone, and the weight would have crushed America ; it was time to act. The Abolition party, or rather the party opposed to the extension of slavery, has acted with a resolution which should excite our sympathies. The future of the United States was at stake ; it knew it, and it struggled in consequence. Remember the efforts essayed four years ago for the election of Mr. Fremont, efforts which would have succeeded perhaps, if Mr. Fremont had not been a Catholic. Remember those three months of balloting, by which the North succeeded in carrying the election of speaker of the House of Representatives. Remember the conduct of the North, in the sad affair of John Brown, its refusal to approve an illegal act, its admiration of the heroic farmer who died after having witnessed the death of his sons. On seeing the public mourning of the Free States, on hearing the minute gun discharged in the capital of the State of New York on the day of execution, one might have foreseen the irresistible impulse which has just ended in the triumph of Mr. Lincoln.

The indignation against slavery, the love of country and of its compromised honor, the just susceptibilities of the North, the liberal instincts so long repressed, the desire of elevating the debased and corrupt institutions of the land, the need of escaping insane projects, the powerful impulse of the Christian faith, all these sentiments contributed, without doubt, to swell the resistance against which the supremacy of the South has just been broken. This, then, is a legal victory, one of the most glorious spectacles that the friends of liberty can contemplate on earth. It was the more glorious, the more efforts and sacrifices it demanded. The Lincoln party had opposed to it, the Puseyistic and financial aristocracy of New York; the manœuvres of President Buchanan were united against it with those of the Southern States. Many of the Northern journals accused it of treading under foot the interests of the seaports, and of compromising the sacred cause of the Union.

To succeed in electing Mr. Lincoln, we must not forget that it was necessary to put the question of principle above the questions of immediate interests, which usually make themselves heard so distinctly. The unity, the greatness of the country, the gigantic future towards which it was advancing, were so many obstacles arising in the way. Then came the reckoning of profits and losses, the inevitable crisis, the Southern orders already withdrawn, the certain loss of money; it seems to me that men who have braved such chances, have nobly accomplished their duty.

America, it is said, is the country of the dollar; the Americans think only of making money, all other considerations are subordinate to this. If the reproach is sometimes well-founded, we must admit, at least, that it is not always so. Those who wish to persuade us that the Abolitionists in this again have simply sought their own interests, by seeking to break down the competition of servile labor, forget two or three things: first, that the slaves produce tobacco or cotton, while the North produces wheat, so that there is not a race in the world that competes less with it: next, that the cotton of the South is very useful to the North, useful to its manufactures, useful to its trade, both transit and commission. The people of the North are not reputed to lack foresight; they were not ignorant that in electing Mr. Lincoln, they had, for the time at least, every thing to lose and nothing to gain; they were not ignorant that Mr. Lincoln occasioned the immediate threat of secession; that the threat of secession was a commercial crisis, was the political weakening of the country, and the unsettling of many fortunes. But neither were they ignorant that above the fleeting interests of individuals and of the nation, arose those permanent interests which must rest only on justice; they decided, cost what it might, to wrest themselves from the detestable, and ere long fatal allurements of the slavery policy.

Let us beware how we calumniate, without intending it, the few generous impulses which break out here and there among mankind. I know that there is a would-be prudent skepticism which attacks all moral greatness that it may depreciate it, all enthusiasm that it may translate it into calculation. To admire nothing is most deplorable, and, I hasten to add, most absurd. Without wandering from the subject of slavery, I can cite the great Emancipation Act, wrested from Parliament by Christian public opinion in England. Have not means been found to prove, or at least to insinuate, that this act, the most glorious of our century, was at the bottom nothing but a Machiavellian combination of interests? Doubtless, those who have taken the trouble to look over the debates of the times know what we are to think of this fine explanation; they know what resistance was opposed by *interests* to the emancipation, both in the colonies and in the heart of the metropolis; they know with how much obstinacy the Tories, representing the traditions of English politics, combated the proposed plans; they know in what terms the certain ruin of the planters, the manufactures, and the seaports, was described; they know by how many petitions the churches, the religious societies, the women, and even the children, succeeded in wresting from Parliament a measure refused by so many statesmen. But the mass of the people do not go back to the beginning; they take for granted the summary judgment that English emancipation was a master-piece of perfidy.

We hear very nearly the same thing said of that glorious movement which has just taken place in America. We would gladly detect all motives in it except one that is generous and Christian. As if a vulgar calculation of interest would not have dictated a contrary course! And it is precisely this that makes the greatness of the resolution adopted by the North. It knew all the consequences; they had been announced by the South, recapitulated by prudent men, stated in detail by the newspapers of great commercial cities; it chose to be just. Despite the inevitable mingling of base and selfish impulses, which always become complicated in such manifestations, the ruling motive in this was a protest of conscience, and of the spirit of liberty.

The accounts that have come to us from America demonstrate the lofty character of the joy which was manifested after the election. Men shook hands with each other in the streets; they congratulated each other on having at last escaped from the yoke of an ignoble policy; they felt as though relieved from a weight; they breathed more freely; the true, the noble destinies of the United States reappeared on the horizon, they saluted a future that should be better than the present, a future worthy of their sires, those early pilgrims who, carrying nothing with them but their Bibles, had laid the foundation of a free country with poor but valiant hands.

I should like to quote here the sermon in which the Rev. Mr. Beecher poured out his Christian joy at that time. He spoke of the strength of the weak; he showed that principles, however despised they may be, end by revenging themselves on interests; he recalled the fact that the Gospel is a power in America. To rise up, to attack its enemy manfully, to arraign the causes of the national decline, to approach boldly the solution of the most formidable problem which could be propounded here on earth, such is not the act of a nation of calculators. Something else is implied in it than tactics, something else than combinations of votes or sectional rivalries. To vote as they did, they had to overcome almost as many obstacles in the North as in the South; for, in consequence of the vote, the North had to suffer like the South, and they knew it.

If you wish to be just to the United States, compare them with other countries in which slavery exists. In the United States there is a struggle; the question is a living one; men do not turn aside from it with lax indifference. I love the noise of free nations; I find in the very violence of their debates a proof of the earnestness of convictions. Men must become excited about great social problems; if abuses exist, they must, at least, be pointed out, attacked, and stigmatized; the prescription of silence must never be accorded them; devoted voices must exclaim against them, unceasingly, in the name of justice and of humanity. Such a spectacle does good to the soul; it solaces the sorrows of the present, it carries within itself guarantees for the future.

The sad, profoundly sad, spectacle, is that of nations where crimes make no noise. Look at Brazil. Like the United States, it has slavery, but it is an honorable, discreet slavery, of which nothing is said.

Whatever may happen there, no one inquires about it; there are no discussions, either through the press or in the courts. No party would dare insert such a question into its platform. One thing, very properly, has been found to disturb it, and the public sale of slaves has just been forbidden.

Look, above all, at Spain and its island of Cuba. There, too, is perfect silence. Nothing, in truth, opposes the belief that Cuba is the abode of felicity, and that the atrocities of slavery are the monopoly of the United States. But inquisitive people, who like to search to the bottom of things, discover that if the masters are very gentle at Havana, the overseers are scarcely so on their account on the plantations; I have already given the proof of it. Out of ten slavers that are seized on the high seas, nine are always destined to Cuba. Spain has forbidden the slave trade; she has even been compensated for it by the English; but this does not prevent her from suffering it to be carried on before her eyes with almost absolute impunity. Her high-sounding phrases change nothing; the smallest fact is of more value. At Cuba, the landing of slaves is continual, and the places of disembarkation are known. Now, the American flag protects no one at the time of disembarking. Why is no opposition made to this?

Why has the importation of negroes tripled in Cuba? Why does no slaver, American or any other, steer towards Brazil, since Brazil has *desired* to put an end to the slave trade? The answer to these questions will be given us on the day when Spain shall *desire*, in turn, to suppress it. In the mean time she prefers to keep silence, unless when a word from London strikes out a concert of protestations more patriotic than convincing; save in this case, the government is silent, public opinion is silent, no colonial sheet is found ready to hazard an objection, nor even a metropolitan journal that is willing to disturb so touching an equanimity. The court of Madrid, in which many questions are agitated, prudently stands aloof in the matter of slavery and the slave trade; among the numerous parties disputing for power, not one dares venture on a ground where it would meet nothing but unpopularity. Ah! after this death-like silence, how the soul is refreshed by the fiery contests of the United States, the great word-combats carried on in every village of the Union, the appeals addressed to the conscience, the battle in broad daylight! How refreshing to see by the side of these nations, who sleep so tranquilly, while regarding the inroads of slavery, a people whom it disquiets, whom it irritates, who refuse to take part in it, and who, rather than conform to the evil, agitate, become divided, and rend themselves perchance with their own hands!

CHAPTER IV.

WHAT WE ARE TO THINK OF THE UNITED STATES.

WE are not just towards the United States. Their civilization, so different from ours, wounds us in various ways, and we turn from them in the ill-humor excited by their real defects, without taking note enough of their eminent qualities. This country, which possesses neither church, nor State, nor army, nor governmental protection; this country, born yesterday, and born under a Puritanic influence; this country, without past history, without monuments, separated from the Middle Ages by the double interval of centuries and beliefs; this rude country of farmers and pioneers, has nothing fitted to please us. It has the exuberant life and the eccentricities of youth; that is, it affords to our mature experience inexhaustible subjects of blame and raillery.

We are are so little inclined to admire it, that

we seek in its territorial configuration for the essential explanation of its success. Is it so difficult to maintain good order and liberty at home when one has immense deserts to people, when land offers itself without stint to the labor of man?—I do not see, for my part, that land is lacking at Buenos Ayres, at Montevideo, in Mexico, or in any of the pronunciamento republics that cover South America. It seems to me that the Turks have room before them, and that the Middle Ages were not suffering precisely from an excess of population when they presented everywhere the spectacle of anarchy and oppression.

Be sure that the United States, which have something to learn of us, have also something to teach us. Theirs is a great community, which it does not become us to pass by in disdain. The more it differs from our own Europe, the more necessary is impartial attention to comprehend and appreciate it. Especially is it impossible for us to form an enlightened opinion of the present crisis, unless we begin by taking into consideration the surroundings in which it has broken out. The nature of the struggle and its probable issue, the difficulties of the present, and the chances of the future, will be clear to us only on condition of our making a study of the United States. A few details will, therefore, be permitted me.

Among the Yankees, the faults are on the surface. I am not one to justify Lynch law, whatever may be the necessities which exist in the Far West. Riots in the United States are cited which have performed their work of fire and devastation, and which no one has dared treat rigorously afterwards, for fear of incurring disgrace from the sovereign people; but I remember, I fancy, that similar things have been seen in Paris itself. We will not, therefore, lay too great stress on them.

One thing that is not seen in Paris, is, unhappily, remarked in America: the general tendency among women to substitute masculine qualities which scarcely befit them, for the feminine qualities which constitute their grace, their strength, and their dignity; thence results a certain something unpleasant and rude which does no credit to the New World. I by no means admire coarseness, and I do not admit that it is the necessary companion of energy; the tone of the journals and of the debates in Congress is often calculated to excite a just reprobation. There is in the United States a levelling spirit, a jealousy of acquired superiority, and, above all, of inherited distinctions, which proceeds from the worst sentiments of the heart. What is graver still, the tender and gentle side of the human soul, such as shines forth in the Gospel, appears too rarely among this people, where the Gospel, notwithstanding, is in honor, but where the labor of a gigantic growth has developed the active instead of the loving virtues; the Americans are cold even when good, charitable and devout.

They may love money, and often concentrate their thoughts on the means of making it; I will not contest this, although I doubt, on seeing what passes among ourselves, whether we have the right to cast the stone at them; especially as American liberality, as I shall presently show, is of a nature to put our parsimony to shame. As to the bankrupt acts, of which American creditors have many times complained, nothing can justify them; yet here again the rôle of pedagogue scarcely becomes us. If more than one American railroad company have taken advantage of a crisis to declare without much dishonor, a suspension of payment, it is not proved that these suspensions of payment must be converted into bankruptcy. If more than one town or more than one county make the half yearly payments of their debts with reluctance, the courts always do fair justice on this ill will; there are some countries, Russia, for instance, where the courts do not do as much. If, in fine, at one time, a number of States failed to keep their engagements, and a single one dared proclaim the infamous doctrine of repudiation, all have since paid, except one State of the extreme South, Mississippi. Once more, are we sure of being in a position to reprove such misdeeds; we, whose governments, anterior to '89, made use, without much scruple, of the fall of stocks, and bankruptcies; we, whose debt, on emerging from the Revolution, took the significant name of *tiers consolidé?*

Let us not forget that the population of the United States has increased tenfold since the close of the last century; they have received immigrants annually, by hundreds of thousands, who have not always been the elite of the Old World. Must not this perpetual invasion of strangers promptly transformed into citizens, have necessarily introduced into the decision of public affairs some elements of immorality? I admire the honorable and religious spirit of the Americans which has been able to assimilate and rule to such a degree these great masses of Irish and Germans. Few countries would have endured a like ordeal as well.

Remark that, in spite of all, public order is maintained without paid troops, (Continental Europe will find it hard to credit this.) Tranquillity reigns in the largest cities of the United States; respect for the law is in every heart; great ballotings take place, millions of excited men await the result with trembling; yet, notwithstanding, not an act of violence is committed. American riots —for some there are—are certainly less numerous than ours; and they have the merit of not being transformed into revolutions.

The greater part of the immigrants remain, of course, in the large cities; here they come almost to make the laws, and here, too, noble causes encounter the most opponents. Mr. Lincoln, to cite an example, received only a minority of suffrages in the city of New York, whilst the unanimity of the country suffrages secured him the vote of the State. Contempt of the colored class, that crime of the North, breaks out most of all in the large cities, and particularly among agglomerations of immigrants; none are harsher to free negroes, it must be admitted, than newly-landed Europeans who have come to seek a fortune in America.

As to crimes, they are numerous only in cities; still the criminal records of the United States appear somewhat full when compared with ours. I know how great a part of this must be assigned to the insufficiency of repression; in America, criminals doubtless escape punishment much oftener than among us. Notwithstanding, there is real security; and a child might travel over the entire West without being exposed to the slightest danger.

M. de Tocqueville has said that morals are infinitely more rigid in North America than elsewhere. This is not, it seems to me, a trifling advantage. Whatever may be the depravity of the seaports, where the whole world holds rendezvous, it remains certain that it does not penetrate into the interior of the country. Open the journals and novels of the United States; you will not find a corrupt page in them. You might leave them all on the drawing-room table, without fearing to call a blush to the brow of a woman, or to sully the imagination of a child.

In the heart of the manufacturing States, model villages are found, in which every thing is combined to protect the artisans of both sexes from the perils that await them in other countries. Who has not heard of the town of Lowell, where farmers' daughters go to earn their dowry, where the labor of the factories brings no dissipation in its train, where the workwomen read, write, teach Sunday-schools, where their morality detracts nothing from their liberty and progress? When I have added that the United States have not a single foundling asylum, it seems to me that I have indicated what we are to think at once of their good morals and good sense.

And let not the Americans be represented as a people at once honest and narrow-minded. If they are still far from our level—and this must necessarily be true, in an artistic and literary point of view—we are not, however, at liberty to despise a country which counts such names as Hawthorne, Longfellow, Emerson, Cooper, Poe, Washington Irving, Channing, Prescott, Motley, and Bancroft. Note that among these names, men of imagination hold a prominent place, which proves, we may say in passing, that the country where we oftenest hear the exclamation, "Of what use is it?" agrees in finding poetry of some use. And I speak here neither of orators, like Mr. Seward or Mr. Douglas, nor of scholars, like Lieutenant Maury, nor of those who, like Fulton or Morse, have applied science to art: judgment has been passed on all these points.

But the true superiority of Americans is in the universality of common instruction. The Puritans, who came hither with their Bibles, were of necessity zealous founders of schools; the Bible and the school go together. See, therefore, what the schools are in the United States! The State of Massachusetts alone, which does not number a million of souls, devotes five millions yearly to its public instruction. If other States are far from equalling it in academies and higher institutions, all are on a level with it as regards primary schools; a man or woman, therefore, is rarely found outside the class of immigrants, who does not possess a solid knowledge of the elementary sciences, the extent of which would excite our surprise. By the side of the primary school, and to complete its instruction in the religious point of view, the Americans have everywhere opened Sunday-schools, kept gratuitously by volunteer teachers, among whom have figured many men of the highest standing, several of whom have been Presidents of the Confederation. These Sunday-schools, not less than twenty thousand in number, and superintended by one hundred and fifty thousand teachers, count more than a million of pupils, of which ten thousand at least are adults. Calculate the power of such an instrument!

People read enormously in America. There is a library in the meanest cabin of roughly-hewn logs, constructed by the pioneers of the West. These poor log-houses almost always contain a Bible, often journals, instructive books, sometimes even poetry. We in Europe, who fancy ourselves fine amateurs of good verses, would scarcely imagine that copies of Longfellow are scattered among American husbandmen. The political journals have many subscribers; those of the religious papers are no less numerous. I know of a monthly journal designed for children, (the *Child's Paper*,) of which three hundred thousand copies are printed. This is the intellectual aliment of the country. In the towns, lectures are added to books, journals, and reviews: in all imaginable subjects, this community, which the Government does not charge itself with instructing, (at least, beyond the primary education,) educates and develops itself with indefatigable ardor. Ideas are agitated in the smallest market-town; life is everywhere.

Accustomed to act for themselves, knowing that they cannot count on the administrative patronage of the State, the Americans excel in bringing individual energies into action. There are few functionaries, few soldiers, and few taxes among them. They know nothing, like us, of that malady of public functions, the violence of which increases in proportion as we advance. They know nothing of those enormous imposts under which Europe is bending by degrees—those taxes which almost suppress property by overburdening its transmission; they have not come to the point of finding it very natural to devote one or two millions every year to the expenses of the State, and no theory has been formed to prove to them that of all the expenses of the citizens, this is applied to the best purpose. They have not entered with the Old World into that rivalry of armaments in which each nation, though it become exhausted in the effort, is bound to keep on a level with its neighbors, and in which no one will be stronger in the end when the whole world shall be subjugated. Their ten thousand regulars suffice, and they have their militia for extraordinary occasions. Lastly, their Federal debt is insignificant; and, if the private debts of a few States reach a high figure, they are nowhere of a nature to impose on the tax-payers a large surplus of charges.

All of the great liberties exist in the United States: liberty of the press, liberty of speech, right of assemblage, right of association. Except in the slave States, where the national institutions have been subjected to deplorable mutilations in fact, every citizen can express his opinion and maintain it openly, without meeting any other obstacle than the contrary opinion, which is expressed with equal freedom.

But there is one ground above all where we should acknowledge the superiority of America: I mean, religious liberty. We are still in the beginning of doubts upon the point as to where the interference of the State should cease; in what measure it should govern the belief of the citizens, and its manifestation. These questions, alas, are still propounded among us. And there are countries at our doors, where men shudder at the mere idea that the law may some day cease to decide for each in what manner he is bound to worship God, that the courts may cease to punish those whose conscience turns aside from the path of the nation. Protestant Sweden but lately condemned dissenters to fine and imprisonment; Catholic Spain daily inflicts the severest penalties on those who suffer themselves to profess or to propagate beliefs which are not those of the country—those who sell the Scriptures, and those who read them.

The United States have not only proclaimed and loyally carried out the glorious principle of religious liberty, but have adopted as a corollary another principle, much more contested among us, but which I believe destined also to make the tour of the world: the principle of separation of Church and State. That believers should support their own worship, that religious and political questions should never be blended, that the two provinces should remain distinct, is a simple idea which seems most strange to us to-day. It will make its way like all other true ideas, which begin as paradoxes and end by becoming axioms. Meanwhile, the American Confederation enjoys an advantage which more than one European government, I suspect, would at some moments purchase at a high price: it has not to trouble itself about religious interests, either in its action without or its administration within. If there are conflicts everywhere in the spiritual order, it leaves them to struggle and become resolved in the spiritual order, without needing to trouble itself in the matter. Hence arises for the State a freedom of bearing, a simplicity of conduct, which we, who have to steer adroitly through so many dangers, can hardly comprehend. The American government is sure of never offending any church—it knows none; it does not interfere either to combat or to aid them; it has renounced, once for all, intervention in the domain of conscience.

The result, doubtless, is, that this domain is not so well ordered as in Europe; the administrative ecclesiastical state has by no means submitted to such regulation. Is that to say that this inconvenience (if it be one) is not largely compensated for by its advantages? Is it nothing to suppress inheritance in religious matters, and to force each soul to question itself as to what it believes? In the United States, adhesion to a church is an individual, spontaneous act, resulting from a voluntary determination. This is so true that four-fifths of the inhabitants of the country do not bear the title of church members. Although attending worship, although manifesting an interest and zeal in the subject to which we are little accustomed, although assiduous church-goers, and liberal givers, they have not yet felt within themselves a conviction strong and clear enough to make a public profession of faith. Think what we may of such a system, we must avow, at least, that it implies a profound respect for sacred things; nothing can less resemble that indolent and formal assent which we give, in conformity with custom, and without binding ourselves, in earnest, to the religion that prevails among us.

Hence arises something valiant in American convictions. Hence arises also, it may be said, that dispersion of sects, the picture of which is so often drawn for us. I am far from loving the spirit of sectarianism, and I am careful not to present the American churches as the beau ideal in religious matters. The sectarian spirit, the fundamental trait of which is to confound unity with uniformity, to transform divergencies into separations, to refuse to admit into the bosom of the church the element of diversity and of liberty; to exact the signing of a theological formula, and the formal adhesion as a whole to a collection of dogmas and practices, without tolerating the slightest shade of difference—the sectarian spirit, with its narrowness, with its traditions of men, with its exaggeration of little things, with its separate denominations, is certainly not worthy of admiration. I reject it in America as elsewhere, but I think it well to state that the religious disruption produced by it has been much exaggerated. We must greatly abbreviate the formidable list of churches furnished us by travellers. Putting aside those which have no value, either as to influence or numbers, we reduce the numbers of denominations existing in the United States, outside the Roman Catholic church, to five, (and these are too many;) namely: Methodist, Baptist, Congregational, Episcopal, and Presbyterian. The remainder is composed of small eccentric congregations which spring up and die, and of which no one takes heed, except a few tourists, who are always willing to note down extraordinary facts.

We will add that the sectarian spirit is now attacked in America, and that the essential unity which binds the members of the five denominations together, in spite of some external differences, is manifesting itself forcibly. Not only does the evangelical alliance prove to the most sceptical that this unity is real, but a fact peculiar to the United States, the great awakening produced by the crisis of 1857, has given evidence of the perfect harmony of convictions. In the innumerable meetings caused to spring up by this awakening from one end of the country to the other, it has been impossible to distinguish Baptists, Presbyterians, or Congregationalists from each other. All have been there, and no one has betrayed by the least shade of dogmatism those self-styled profound divisions about which so much noise is made. I invite those still in doubt to look at the manner in which public worship is established in the West: as soon as a few men have formed a settlement, a missionary comes to visit them; no one inquires about his denomination, for the Bible that he brings is the Bible of all, and the salvation, through Christ, which he proclaims, is the faith of all. It suffices, besides, to see this entire people, so restless, so laborious, leaving its business on Sunday to occupy itself with the thoughts of another life; it suffices to observe the unanimous uprising of the public conscience at the rumor of an attack directed against the Gospel, to perceive that unity subsists beneath lamentable divisions, and that individual conviction creates the most active of all cohesive powers in the heart of human communities; I know of no cement that equals it.

If individual convictions are a strong bond, they are also an inexhaustible source of life. It is easy to assure ourselves of this by a brief survey of the proofs of Christian liberality which are displayed in the United States. Here, there is no legal charity, no aid to be expected from the government, either for the support of churches, or for that of the sick and poor; the *voluntary system* must suffice for all. And, in fact, it does suffice for all.

What is the first thing in question? To collect thirty million francs annually for the payment of the clergy. The thirty millions are furnished: poor and rich, all give eagerly, and without compulsion. The next thing in question is to provide for the construction of new churches; now, it is necessary to finish not less than three of these daily, for the clearing of the forests advances with rapid strides, and a thousand churches, at least, are built every year. The majority of these churches are doubtless composed of beams laid one upon another, then painted white, or left of the natural color, and surmounted by a bell; they are simple and inexpensive, and, in the infant villages, the streets of which are still blocked up by trees left standing, the place, serving at once for a church and a school, where the people gather round an itinerant preacher, is not decorated with much sumptuousness; yet these new edifices demand annually from twelve to fifteen millions.

Next come the religious societies. In the West, preachers are needed, hardy laborers, who live in privations, traversing vast solitudes on horseback, and journeying continually, without repose, until their strength is exhausted. Eight hundred missionaries or agents are required for the American Board of Missions, for the Presbyterians, the Baptists, and all the other churches. Now, they cannot send them to the four quarters of the globe without providing for their wants. The Bible Society, which prints three hundred thousand Bibles annually, the Religious Tract Society, which publishes every year five millions of tracts, and which, in New York alone, employs a thousand visitors or distributors; the various works, in a word, expend from nine to ten million francs.

Such, then, is the budget of voluntary charity in the United States.* It amounts to fifty or sixty million francs, without counting the very considerable donations destined to public instruction; without counting (and this is immense) the relief of the sick and the poor. You will scarcely find a village in the whole United States that has not its benevolent society, and private benevolence, which is the best, also carries on its work, independently of societies. I know of no country where acts of profuse liberality are more frequent; one man founds a hospital, another an observatory. Asylums are opened for all human unfortunates, for lunatics, the blind, the deaf, orphans, abandoned children.

Was I not right in saying that this is a great people? Whatever may be its vices, we are not at

* It seems that I have understated the truth; but I prefer to do so; I wish, above all, to avoid exaggeration.

liberty to speak of it with disdain. If the Americans know how to make a fortune, they know, also, how to make a noble use of their fortune; accused with reason, as they are, of being too often preoccupied with questions of profit, we have seen them retrenching much of their luxury since the commercial crisis, yet economizing very little in their charities. The budget of the churches and religious societies remained intact at the very time that embarrassment was everywhere prevailing. I cannot help believing that there are peculiar blessings attached to so many voluntary sacrifices which carry back the mind to the early ages of Christianity. We may be sure that the religion that costs something, brings something also in return.

CHAPTER V.

THE CHURCHES AND SLAVERY.

This leads me to examine a side of the American question upon which attention is naturally fixed at the present time; how is it that the iniquities of slavery are maintained among this charitable and liberal people? how is it that such iniquities have subsisted under the influence of so powerful a Christian sentiment? Can it be true that Christians have deserted the cause of justice? Has the Gospel had the place which belongs to it, in the great struggle that is going on between the North and the South? yes; or no. This is perhaps the point of all others most important to clear up; first, because it is the one on which the most errors have accumulated; next, because it is the one most closely connected with the final solution; for this solution will not be happy, if the Gospel has no hand in it.

To judge rightly, let us approach and endeavor

to comprehend the true position of those whose conduct we seek to appreciate. See the South, for example, where the almost universal opinion is favorable to slavery, where governors write dithyrambics on its benefits, where many Christians have succeeded in discovering that it is sanctioned by the Gospel, where men of sincerity are now placing their impious crusades in behalf of its extension under the protection of God, where numerous preachers expound in their own way the celebrated text "Cursed be Canaan!" Do not these sentiments of the South, detestable as they are, find, to a certain point, their explanation and excuse in the circumstances in which the South is placed?

The power of surroundings is incalculable. If we ourselves, who condemn slavery, and are right in so doing, had been reared in Charleston; if we had led a planter's life from our earliest infancy; if we had nourished our minds with their ideas; if we considered our monetary interests menaced by Abolitionism; if the image of more fearful perils, of violent destructions and massacres, appeared to haunt our thoughts; if the political antagonism between the North and the South came to add its venom to the passions already excited within us, is it certain that we ourselves should not be figuring at the present time among the desperadoes who are firing upon the ships of the Union, and attempting the foundation of a Southern Confederacy?

It is well to ask this of ourselves, in order to learn to respect, to love, and consequently to aid those whose conduct we blame the most strongly. For my part, whenever I am tempted to set myself up as a judge or an accuser of the South, I ask myself what I should do if I belonged to the South, and this brings me back to the true position. I remember, too, what I saw, with my own eyes, at the time when the discussion on slavery was carried on in France; the colonial passions, the blindest and most violent of all, broke out in Martinique and the isle of Bourbon, as they had broken out before in Jamaica, where the circulars of Mr. Canning, the proposition, for example, to suppress the flagellation of women, had excited a veritable explosion. There were some very honorable men among those who were indignant at this measure; and, among us, likewise, the planters who determined to combat all modification of the negro system, were good men. Severity is almost always a defect of memory; we blame others without pity, only when we begin by forgetting our own history. We Frenchmen, who had so much difficulty in emancipating our own slaves, and who would not, perhaps, have succeeded in it, had it not been for the bold decision of M. Schoelcher; we, who have sought to take back, in part, through our colonial regulations, the liberty accorded the blacks; we, who suffered recruitals by purchase to be made on the African coast; who formerly organized the expedition charged with re-establishing slavery and the slave trade at St. Domingo; who suppressed the slave trade at the Congress of Vienna only in stipulating its continuance for some years; who carried into our discussions on the right of search, a very meagre interest for the victims of the slavers; we, whose consciences are burdened with these misdeeds, are bound to use indulgence towards the States of the South.

This remark was necessary: it is from the South that the Biblical theories in favor of slavery proceed; it is on account of the South that these theories have been adopted by certain Christians of the North, desirous, above every thing, of avoiding both the dismemberment of the United States, and that of the churches and religious societies. Take away the South, and no one in America, any more than in Europe, will dream of discovering in the

Gospel the divine approbation of the atrocities of slavery.

I comprehend better than most, the sentiment of indignation that is caused by these deplorable teachings, in which slavery is sometimes excused, sometimes exalted ; I comprehend, that, under the impulse of a sentiment so justifiable, one may be led on to anathematize preachers and churches in a mass, that he may even come to the point of representing to himself the Christian faith as the true obstacle to the progress of liberty. This is a great perversion of the truth, but we can easily understand how it has succeeded in gaining the assent of generous and sincere minds. I myself have read a sermon which was listened to with sympathy in a certain Presbyterian church in New York, in which slavery, declares right until the return of Jesus Christ, ceases to be so, I know not why, during the millennium ? I know the nature of that theology, too truly styled *cottony*, which is displayed in the clerical columns of the *New York Observer*. Notwithstanding, I hasten to say that these revolting excesses seldom appear except in seaports, and especially in New York. The interests of this great city are bound up to such a degree with those of the cotton States, that, until very lately, New York might have been considered as a prolongation of the South. We need not be surprised, therefore, to find some congregations there which are ruled by the prejudices of the South. Besides, even in New York, other churches protest with holy zeal, and other journals, among which I will cite the *Independent*, the organ of the Congregationalists, combat slavery unceasingly in the name of the Gospel.

Then people persist in seeing only New York, in taking notice only of what passes in New York; but they forget that New York is ordinarily an exception in the North, as much by its commercial position as by its opinions and votes. Let us go ever so short a distance from the city into the surrounding country, and we will encounter a different spirit—a spirit thoroughly impregnated with Christian faith, and little disposed to covenant with slavery. There we begin to see that race of Puritan farmers, but lately represented by John Brown. Has not the attempt been made to transform him also into a free thinker, a philosophic enemy of the Bible, and, from this very cause, an enemy to slavery? We need nothing more than his last letter to his wife, to show from what source he had drawn that courage, so misdirected but so indomitable, which he displayed at Harper's Ferry; the Christian, the

Biblical and orthodox Christian, comes to explain the liberal and the hero.

That Christians in general condemned the enterprise of John Brown, while sympathizing with him, I hasten to acknowledge; and I am far from blaming them. That many have committed the real wrong of recoiling before the consequences of an open and decided conduct, I am forced to admit. Yes, without even mentioning the South, where, as every one knows, the reign of terror prevails, there are numerous Protestant and Catholic churches in the remainder of the Confederation, which have refused to declare themselves, as they should have done, in opposition to the crime of slavery. Let us not hasten, however, to cry out against falsehood and hypocrisy; most honorable and sincere men have believed that they would do more harm than good by bringing on a rupture with the South. Let us not forget that political rupture is complicated here with religious rupture. Now, all the churches extend over both North and South; all the charitable societies number committees and subscribers in both North and South. The point in question then, (let us weigh the immensity of the sacrifice,) the point in question is to rend in twain all the churches, to break in pieces all the societies, to expose to perilous risks all the great works that do honor to the United States.

Doubtless, to have gone their way, to have done their duty, and not to have troubled themselves about the consequences, was the great rule of action. I grant it; yet, notwithstanding, I refuse to stigmatize, as many have done, those men who have committed the fault of hesitating; I feel that to rank them among the champions of slavery is to pervert facts, and to fall into a blamable exaggeration. Again, to-day, after the election of Mr. Lincoln, cannot citizens be cited in the North who are devoted to the cause of the negroes, but who refuse to participate in abolitionist demonstrations, because they fear (and the sentiments does them honor) to encourage the impending insurrections?

This said, I wish to prove by some too well-known facts, what has been this forbearance, or even this pretended hesitation of orthodox Christianity. On regarding the churches, I see two, and the most considerable, which have openly declared themselves: the Congregationalists and the Methodists. About six months since, the General Conference of Methodists resolutely plunged into the current without suffering itself to be trammelled by the protests which came to it from the South.

I read in a report presented to one of the great divisions of this church: "We believe that to sell or to hold in bondage human beings under the name of chattels, is in contradiction to the divine laws and to humanity; and that it conflicts with the golden rule and with the rule of our discipline." Last year, a numerous assemblage of delegates of the Congregational churches adopted the following resolution: "Slaveholding is immoral, and slaveholders should not be admitted as members of Christian churches. We ought to protest against it without ceasing, in the name of the Gospel, until it shall have entirely disappeared." And this resolution has not remained a dead letter: a Congregational church of Ohio has expelled from its bosom one of its deacons, who had contributed in the capacity of magistrate to the extradition of a fugitive slave.

Other churches, without taking so decided a position, have at least manifested by their internal convulsions the profound interest excited among them by the question of slavery. In this manner a secession has just rent the Presbyterian church in twain, because the declared adversaries of slavery were unwilling to remain responsible for a forbearance which appeared to them criminal. These things are signs of life, and these signs are beginning to show themselves even in the midst of ecclesiastical bodies which have acted, until now, in the most unchristian manner. A warm discussion has been thus called forth, and this signifies a great deal, among the members of the Episcopal church in New York. The majority stifled the debate; will it be able to do this always?

If from the churches we proceed to the religious societies, we find the same symptoms among them; here, they declare themselves openly against slavery, in spite of the menaces of the South; there, they succeed in staving off the question, yet at the price of excited debates, which continually spring up again, of a great scandal, and of protests which are heard by Christians through the whole world. The course of conduct adopted by the great American Board of Missions is the more significant, inasmuch as its committee is composed of members belonging to various evangelical denominations; it stands, therefore, as their permanent representative, yet this has not prevented its adoption, after long hesitation, of resolutions indicating in what course it will henceforth proceed: it has broken off its relations with the missonaries employed among the Choctaws, for the sole reason that they obstinately refused openly to attack Indian slavery, and the abominable practices which it engenders. The Society, which long, too long, contented itself with a timid and inconsistent censure, has been obliged, therefore, to resort to more decisive measures.

Another great body, the Tract Society, unfortunately, has not followed this example; the general assemblies held at New York, and ruled by the spirit of that city, have given a majority to the party opposed to the discussion of the subject; but, be it said to the honor of American Christians, the very large minority resisted to the end; the latter was sustained by outside opinion, and many friends of the Gospel joined with it in deploring the pusillanimity which yielded to the menaces of the South. A crisis thence arose, which has not yet reached its height, and the first fruits of which have been the foundation of a rival society in Boston, to which adherents are gathering from all sides.

These are grave events, for they manifest the inmost revolutions of the human soul. Would you know what will take place in political societies? Begin by informing yourself about what is taking place in the consciences of the public. Now it is evident that the public conscience is in motion in the United States. The vast obstacles by which this movement was trammelled have been surmounted on every side. I wish no other proof of this than the deplorable fact of which I have just made mention: the conduct of the Tract Society, the internal crisis which it has experienced, the reprobation which it encounters in Europe as in America. Are not these palpable proofs of the too little known truth that the great moral force which is struggling with American slavery is the Gospel?

And how could it be otherwise? If we had not positive facts before our eyes, if we did not know that one entire sect of Christians, the Quakers, have devoted themselves, body and goods, to the service of poor fugitive slaves, if we did not recognize the deep Puritan imprint in the movement which has colonized Kansas, and in that which has borne Mr. Lincoln to the presidency, should we not be forced to ask ourselves whether it is possible that the Gospel remains a stranger to a struggle undertaken for liberty? There exist, thank God, between liberty and the Gospel, close, eternal, and indestructible relations. I know of one species of freedom which contains the germ of all the rest—freedom of soul; now what was it, if not the Gospel, that introduced this freedom into the world? Remember ancient Paganism: neither liberty of conscience, nor liberty of individuals, nor liberty of families—such was its definition. The State laid its hand upon all the inmost part of existence, the creeds of the fathers, and the education of the children; moral slavery also existed everywhere, and if slavery, properly called, had been anywhere wanting, it would have given cause for astonishment. The Gospel came, and with it these new phenomena: individual belief, true independence makes its advent here on earth, a liberty worthy of the name appears finally among men. From this time we see men lifting up their heads, despotism finding its limits, the humblest, the weakest opposing to it insurmountable barriers.

They act without reflection, who attempt to place in opposition these two things: the Gospel and liberty. And remark that in the United States, in particular, the Gospel and liberty are accustomed to go together; they first landed together at New Plymouth with the passengers of the Mayflower. Why had these poor pilgrims torn themselves from all the habits of home and country, to seek in the dead of winter an asylum on an unknown soil? Because they loved the Gospel, and because they desired liberty; the chief of liberties—that of the conscience. From the 21st of December, 1620, there existed on the shores of the New World the beginning of a free people—free through the powerful influence of the Gospel. All who have studied the United States with sincerity, will ratify the opinion of M. de Tocqueville: "America is the place, of all others, where the Christian religion has preserved the most power over souls." This power is such, that we find it at the base of all lasting reforms. In this country, in which the idea of authority has little force, there is one authority, that of the Bible, before which the majority bow, and which is of the more importance inasmuch as it alone commands respect and obedience.

If you doubt the decisive part which the Gospel fills in American debates, look at the pains taken by parties to render public homage to it, the Democrats as the Republicans, Mr Buchanan as Mr. Lincoln. Then look more closely at the Republican party, do you not find in it again the visible traces of Puritanism? It is the ancient States, it is old America, it is also the Young America of the farmers, of the pioneers of the Western solitudes, the America of the clearers of the forests, the America of the Bible and the schools. This America long since abolished slavery, and prevented its introduction into the territories that acknowledged its influence. In the meanest of its cabins, you will find the Scriptures, hymn books, reports of religious societies; in the majority of its families, domestic worship is celebrated; in its prayer-meetings, it is not rare to see physicians, lawyers, magistrates, marine officers, taking part publicly; its statesmen do not think themselves dishonored by keeping a Sunday-school; the Gospel, in a word, is a power to which no other can compare, and outside of which it would be puerile to expect to succeed in accomplishing any thing of importance.

Here the action of the Gospel can be plainly detected; an important religious event preceded and paved the way for the political event which we have witnessed: before the election of Mr. Lincoln, an awakening took place. The American awakening, which must not be confounded with those *revivals*, the description and sometimes the caricature of which have been transmitted us by travellers, the awakening, which had neither ecstasies nor convulsive sobs, and the distinctive feature of which was a tone of simplicity and conviction, produced one of those profound agitations of the conscience, which give rise to generous resolutions. The financial crisis had just overthrown the fortunes of the people; they turned towards God and began to pray. On a route of three thousand miles, wherever one might stop, he found a meeting, a simple, spontaneous meeting, at which the pastors did not take the initiative, where they were present instead of presiding. Ere long, public attention became fixed on this movement, the greatness of which could not be contested; the most hostile journals ended by rendering it homage. And it lasted, it still subsists, it has produced something else than meetings and prayers, it has induced extensive moral reforms, it has closed places of debauchery and taverns by hundreds. The military and commercial marine of the United States has been especially subjected to its influence; captains, officers, and sailors in great numbers, have shown by their lives that their habits of piety are more than a vain form; American vessels are perhaps the only ones at the present day in which groups of sailors assemble to converse on the interests of their soul, and to make the praises of God resound over the ocean.

In strengthening the religious element, in exciting the Puritan fibre of America, the awakening certainly contributed a great share to the success of the party opposed to slavery. South Carolina acknowledged this herself lately, when she inserted the following phrase in her declaration of independence: "The public opinion of the North has given to a great political error the sanction of a still more erroneous religious sentiment." Is this religious sentiment, assailed by the slaveholders, that of free thinkers, or of Christians? The South is not mistaken; it knows that the truly difficult acts of emancipation are accomplished on earth only by the power of the Gospel; it saw the great abolition impulse rise in England, and spread over the United States; journals, committees, correspondence, all indicated that the English had become the American movement, and was continued under the same banner. Under this banner, and this alone, it has conquered. A colossal work in fact is here in question, before which all purely human forces fall to the ground. If such prodigious Christian efforts were needed to give the victory to Wilberforce, what will be required in the heart of a country where slavery is not exiled to distant colonies, and where it has acquired formidable proportions with years. There are easy abolitions, which are wrought in some sort of themselves, and which seem the natural corollary of a political revolution; as, for instance, that which occurred forty years ago in the Spanish republics. Bolivar, Quiroga, and the other leaders, needed the support of all classes of the population in their struggle against Spain; they adopted the expedient of suppressing slavery. In taking this resolution, they accomplished a most honorable deed, but they made little change in the condition of the country, for large planting was rare, and both the blacks and the whites were few in numbers, less numerous, indeed, than the Indians and the half breeds.

If political reasons then sufficed, it is evident that they are far from sufficing to-day: we must seek elsewhere for the explanation of the movement which, a long time wavering and suppressed, has just manifested its irresistible power in the United States. We have recognized in it the hand of the Gospel; and this is no indifferent matter, for if the Gospel had no part in it, such a movement would end in destruction.

The responsibility of Christians will be great in America; they can do much for the favorable solution of a problem which menaces the future of their country, and overshadows that of humanity. The mode of pacification here is, to declare themselves; the pretensions of the South, its fatal progress, the extreme peril to which but lately it exposed the Confederation, are due much more than is imagined to the deplorable hesitation of the religious societies and the churches. If it had long since been brought face to face with a determined evangelical doctrine, the

South, which knows also, though in a less degree, the influence of the Gospel, would have avoided falling into the excesses to which it is now abandoned. The faults of the past are irreparable, but it is possible to ward off their return. Let all Northern churches, let all societies, let all eminent Christians take henceforth with firmness the position which they ought to have taken from the first; let them present to their Southern brethren a solid rallying point, and the effects of this faithful conduct will not be slow in making themselves felt. There is, in the slave States, especially in those occupying an intermediate position, more disturbance of thought, and more conflicts of feeling, than we generally suppose. Let the banner of the Christian faith be openly displayed, and many good men will rally round it: this is certain.

And let no one put forward the shameful pretext: there are sceptics, rationalists, free thinkers in the ranks of Abolitionism! Why not? Questions of this sort, thanks to the Gospel, have entered in the domain of common morality, shall I desert these questions in order to avoid contact with men who reject the essential doctrines of Christianity? I confess that the orthodoxy which should draw such conclusions would appear suspicious to me.

Voltaire pleading for the Calas will not make me turn my back on religious liberty; Channing writing pages against slavery, revealing a heart more Christian than his doctrine; Parker, blending his noble efforts in favor of the negroes with his assaults against the Bible, will not alienate me from a cause which was mine before it was theirs.

I say, besides, that the objections of these men against Christianity force me to ask whether our conduct as Christians be not one of the principal causes of their scepticism. Is it quite certain that Voltaire himself would have been the adversary that we know him, if he had not seen that thought was stifled, that liberty was crushed, that conscience was violated in the name of the Gospel? Would not this same Gospel have presented itself under a different aspect to Parker, Channing, and the other Unitarians of Boston, if they had seen it at its post, the post of honor, at the head of all generous ideas and true liberties? Yes; there are Abolitionists who reject the Bible because they have heard certain orthodox Christians maintain that the Bible is in favor of slavery. Whoever preaches this, is of a school of impiety.

CHAPTER VI.

THE GOSPEL AND SLAVERY.

How did they set to work to preach this? I will answer this question by two others: How did Bossuet set to work to write his *Politique tirée de l'Ecriture*, to proclaim in the name of the Bible obligatory monarchy, divine right, the absolute authority of kings, the duty of destroying false religion by force, the duty of officially sustaining the truth, the duty of having a budget of modes of worship, the duty of uniting Church and State, without speaking of his Biblical apology for war, for the use of Louis XIV.? How did certain doctors among the Roundheads, in their turn, set to work to proclaim the divine right of republics, and to ordain the massacre of the new Amalekites? The method is very simple: it consists only in confounding the law with the Gospel. This confusion once wrought, the political and civil institutions of the Old Testament lose their temporary and local character, and we go to the New Testament in search of what is not there: namely, political and civil institutions.

Though the Gospel is not the law, it is a truth which has been making its way since the seventeenth century, and which seems to be no longer contested to-day, except in the camp of the champions of slavery. The Gospel, which addresses itself to all nations and all ages, does not pretend to force them into the strait vestments of the ancient Jewish nation; no more does it pretend to "sew a piece of new cloth on an old garment, else the new cloth taketh away from the old, and the rent is made worse." I speak here with a view to those who, in the law as in the Gospel, in the New Testament as in the Old, venerate the infallible word of God. A revelation, to be divine, does not cease to be progressive, and nothing exacts that all truths should be promulgated in a single day. If God deemed proper to give to his people, so long as they needed it, a legislation adapted to their social condition, this legislation, divinely given at that time, may be also divinely abrogated afterward. And this is what has taken place. Those who quote to us texts from the Old Testament concerning slavery, appear to have forgotten the saying of Jesus Christ in reference to another institution, divorce: "It was on account of the hardness of your hearts." Yes, on account of the hardness of their hearts, God established among the Israelites, incapable, at that time, of rising higher, provisory regulations,* perfect as regards his condescension, but most imperfect, as he declares himself, as regards the absolute truth. He who makes no account of this great fact will find in the books of Moses, and in the Prophets, pretexts either for practising to-day what was tolerated only for a time, or for attacking the Scriptures, indignant at what they contain.

It was Jesus Christ himself, therefore, who drew the line of demarcation between the law and the Gospel—who announced the end of local and temporary institutions. Has he revealed other institutions, this time definitive? To form such an idea of the Gospel, we must never have opened it. The Gospel is not a Koran. In the Koran, we doubtless find both civil and criminal laws, and the prin-

* These provisory and imperfect regulations appear none the less admirable when compared, not only with the systems of legislation of other nations of antiquity, but with those which prevail to-day even in the Southern States. According to the law of Moses, the Jewish slave always becomes free in seven years; the foreign slave also becomes free when his master wounds him in chastising him; he has the right to testify in law; he has the right to acquire and to possess.

ciples of government; the Apostles did not once tread on this ground. Fancy what their work would have been, had they substituted a social for a spiritual revolution—had they touched, above all, the question of slavery, which formed part of the fundamental law of the ancient world. And here I wish my thought to be clearly comprehended: I do not pretend that the Apostles were conscious of the unlawfulness of slavery, and that they avoided pointing it out through policy, for fear of compromising their work. No, indeed, this happened unconsciously. According to all appearances, they held the opinions of their times, and God revealed nothing to them on the subject, wishing that the abolition of slavery, like all the social results of the Gospel, should be produced by moral agency, which works from within outward, which changes the heart before changing the actions.

At the time of the Apostles, there were many other abuses than slavery; they never wrote a word in their condemnation. They make allusions to war, yet say nothing of the nameless horrors which then attended it; they speak of the sword placed in the king's hands to punish crime, yet say nothing of those atrocious tortures, in the first rank of which must be cited crucifixion; they make use of figures borrowed from the public games, yet say nothing either of the combats of the gladiators, or of the abominations which sullied other spectacles; they unceasingly call to mind the reciprocal relations of husbands and wives, of parents and children, yet say nothing of the despotic authority which the Roman law conferred upon the father, or of the debasement to which it condemned the wife. The evangelical method is this: it has not occupied itself with communities, yet has wrought the profoundest of the social revolutions; it has not demanded any reform, yet has accomplished all of them; the atrocities of war and of torture, the gladiatorial combats and immodest spectacles, the despotism of fathers and the debasement of women, all have disappeared before a profound, internal action, which attacks the very roots of the evil.

Not only does the Gospel forbear to touch on social and religious problems, but, even on questions of morals, it refuses to furnish detailed solutions. Its system of morality is very short; and in this lies its greatness, through this it becomes morality instead of casuistry. Cases of conscience, special directions, a moral code, promulgated article by article—you will find in it nothing of this sort. What you will find there, and there alone, is a growing morality, which passes my expression. Two or three sayings were written eighteen centuries ago, and these sayings contain in the germ a series of commandments, of transformation, of progression, which we have not nearly exhausted. I spoke a moment since of the progress of revelations; I must speak now of the progress which is being wrought in virtue of a revelation constantly the same, but constantly becoming better understood, which multiplies our duties in proportion as it enlightens our conscience. With the one saying: "What ye would that men should do unto you, do ye also to them," the Gospel has opened before us infinite vistas of moral development.

Before this one saying, the cruelties and infamous customs of ancient society, not mentioned by the Apostles, have successively succumbed; before this one saying, the modern family has been formed; before this one saying, American slavery will disappear as European slavery has disappeared already. With this saying, we are all advancing, we are learning, and we shall continue to learn. Yes, the time will come, I am convinced, when we shall see new duties rise up before us, when we cannot with a clear conscience maintain customs, what, I know not, which we maintain conscientiously to-day.

This carries us somewhat further, it must be granted, than a list of fixed duties *ne varietur;* it opposes slavery in a different manner than a sentence pronounced once for all. The Gospel took the surest means of overthrowing it when, letting alone the reform of institutions, it contented itself with pursuing that of sentiments; when it thus prepared the time when the slaveholder himself would be forced to ask what is contained in the inexhaustible saying: "What ye would that men should do unto you, do ye also unto them." Even in the heart of the Southern States, despite the triple covering of habits, prejudices, and interests, this saying is making its way, and is disturbing the consciences of the people much more than is generally believed. And the work that it has begun it will finish; it will force the planters to *translate* the word SLAVERY, to consider one by one the abominable practices which constitute it. Is it to do to others as we would that they should do to us, to sell a family at retail? To maintain laws which give over every slave, whether wife or maiden, to her owner, whatever he may be, and which take away from this maiden, from this wife, the *right* of remembering her modesty and her duties—what do Christians call this? To produce marketable negroes, to dissolve marriages, to ordain adulteries, to inflict ignoble punishment, to interdict instruction—is this doing to others what we would that they should do to us?

The Christian sense of right is relentless, thank God; it does not suffer itself to be deceived by appearances; where we dispute about words, it forces us to go to facts. Now, look at the facts which are really in question in America, when the great subject of slavery is discussed there theoretically. Against the great evangelical system of morality, the Judaical interpretations of such or such a text have little chance. The epistle of Paul, sending back to Philemon his fugitive slave Onesimus, is quoted to us. Assuredly, the Apostle pronounces in it no anathema against slavery, nor does he exact enfranchisement; these ideas were unknown to him; but he says: "I beseech thee for my son whom I have begotten in my bonds, whom I have sent again: thou therefore receive him, that is my own bowels. Without thy mind would I do nothing; that thy benefit should not be as it were of necessity, but willingly. For perhaps he therefore departed for a season, that thou shouldest receive him forever; not now as a servant, but above a servant, a brother beloved. Having confidence in thy obedience I wrote unto thee, knowing that thou wilt do also more than I say."

Does any one fancy Philemon treating Onesimus, after this epistle, as fugitive slaves are treated in America, putting up his wife and children directly after for sale, or delivering him over to the first slave merchant that was willihg to take charge of him, and carry him a hundred leagues away? It is so certain that Philemon did more than had been told him, that the Epistle to the Colossians shows us the "faithful and well-beloved brother Onesimus" honorably mentioned among those concerned about the spiritual interests of the church.

Do what one will, there is an implied abolition of slavery (implied but positive) at the bottom of that close fraternity created by the faith in the Saviour. Between *brethren*, the relation of master and slave, of merchant and merchandise, cannot long subsist. To sell on an auction-block or deliver over to a slave-driver an immortal soul, for which Christ has died, is an enormity before which the Christian sense of right will always recoil in the end. "In this," it is written, "there is neither Greek nor Jew, nor circumcision nor uncircumcision, nor barbarian nor Scythian, nor bond nor free, but Christ is all and in all." Let slaveholders put to themselves the question what they would say to-day if the epistle to Philemon were addressed to them; and it is addressed to them; the Onesimuses of the South—and such there are—are thus thrown upon the conscience of their masters, their brothers.

I have said enough on the subject to dispense with examining very numerous passages in which slavery is *supposed* by the writers of the New Testament. The duties of masters and of slaves are laid down by them without doubt, and the existence of the institution is not contested for a moment; only, it is brought face to face with that which will slay it: the doctrine of salvation through Christ, of pardon, of humility, of love, is, in itself, and without the necessity of expressing it, the absolute negation of slavery.

It has fully proved so, and the early ages of Christianity leave no doubt as to the interpretation given by Christians to the teachings of the Apostles. Despite the rapid corruptions introduced into the churches, we see one brilliant fact shining forth in them: emancipations becoming more frequent, slaves, as well as free men, succeeding to ecclesiastical offices, spiritual equality producing the fruit which it cannot help producing, namely, legal equality. Observe, too, how the edicts of the emperors multiplied as soon as the influence of Christianity was exerted in the Roman world. And all these edicts had but one aim: to sweeten servitude, to increase affranchisement by law, to facilitate voluntary emancipation.

What the Gospel did then against European slavery, it is doing now against American slavery. Its end is the same; its weapons are the same; they have not rusted during eighteen centuries. Those planters of the English islands were not mistaken, who, instinctively divining where lay their great enemy, had recourse to every measure to expel missionaries from among them. Neither were those Texan executioners mistaken, who lately put to death the missionary Bewley, a touching martyr to the cause of the slaves. I ask, in the face of the gallows of Bewley, what we are to think of that prodigious paradox according to which the Gospel is the patron of slavery. To those who mistake its meaning on this point, the Gospel replies by its acts; it replies also by the unanimous testimony of its servants. What is more striking, in fact, than to see that, apart from the country in which the action of interests and habits disturbs the judgment of Christians, there is but one way of comprehending and interpreting the Scripture on this point? Consult England, France, Germany; Christians everywhere will tell you that the Gospel abolished slavery, although it does not say a single word which would proclaim this abolition. Why, if the doubt were possible, would not diversity of opinions be also possible among disinterested judges? To speak only of France, see the synods of our free churches, which continually stigmatize both Swedish intolerance and American slavery; see an address signed three years ago by the pastors and the elders of five hundred and seventy-one French churches, which has gone to carry to the United States the undoubted testimony of a conviction which in truth is that of all.

It seems to me that our demonstration is complete. What would it be if I should add that American slavery, which its friends so strangely claim to place under the protection of the Apostles, has nothing in common with that of which the Apostles had cognizance. The thing, however, is certain. Slavery, in the United States, is founded on color, it is *negro* slavery. Now, this is a fact wholly new in the history of mankind, a monstrous fact, which profoundly modifies the nature of slavery. Before Las Casas, that virtuous creator of the slave trade, the name of which comprises to him alone a whole commentary on the maxim "Do evil that good may come," before Las Casas, no one had thought of connecting slavery with race. Now, the slavery connected with race is that of all others most difficult to uproot, for it bears an indelible sign of inequality, a sign which the law did not create, and which it cannot destroy.

Such was not the slavery that offered itself to the eyes of the Prophets and Apostles; a normal servitude, of right, based upon a native and indestructible inferiority was not then in question, but an accidental servitude among equals, to which the chances of war had given birth, and which emancipation suppressed entire. Quite different is the slavery which depends on race, and which, it may be said, supposes a malediction; do what one will, this latter will subsist, it will, in a manner, survive itself; it will find, besides, in the idea of a providential dispensation, the natural excuse for its excesses. This slavery the Bible condemns in the most explicit manner. If its champions dare suppose two species, the book of Genesis shows them all mankind springing from one man, and the Gospel recounts to them the redemption wrought in behalf of all the descendants of Adam; if they argue from the curse pronounced against Canaan, the Old Testament presents to them the detailed enumeration of the Canaanites, a vast family, in which the whites figure as well as the blacks.

In short, there is a deadly struggle between the Gospel and slavery under all its forms, and particularly under the odious form which the African slave trade has given it in modern times. The Gospel has been, is, and will be, at the head of every earnest movement directed against slavery. It is important that it should be so; it is the only means of avoiding the acts of violence, the revolts, the extreme calamities from which the whites and the blacks would equally suffer. The Gospel is admirable, inasmuch as by the side of the duties of masters, it proclaims those of slaves; as in the time of the Apostles, it does not hesitate to recommend to them gentleness, submission, scrupulous fidelity, love for those who maltreat them, the practice of difficult virtues; it makes them free within, in order to render them capable of becoming free without.

To judge of this method, we have only to compare the miserable population of St. Domingo with the beautiful free villages which cover the English islands. How true the saying: "The wrath of man never accomplishes the justice of God." Wherever the wrath of man has had full sway, even to chastise abominable abuses, it has remained a curse. I tremble when I think of the revolts which may break out at any moment in the Southern States. Bloodshed, let us not forget, would sully our banner; to the right of the slaves, such a crisis would be forever opposed, and who knows whether a terrible return might not burst upon them?

The mind becomes troubled at the mere image of the horrors that would ensue from civil war. May the Christians of America comprehend, at length, in a more perfect manner, the greatness of the part that God reserves for them, and the extent of the responsibilities that are weighing upon them. To take a stand frankly against slavery; to remove their last pretexts from sincere men who seek to reconcile it with the Gospel; to organize in the North the action of a vast moral power; to address to the South words breathing forth truth and charity; to appeal without wearying to the hearts of masters and slaves; to prepare for trying moments that guarantee which nothing can replace, the common faith of the blacks and the whites; to keep courage even when all seems lost; to practise the Christian vocation, which consists in pursuing and realizing the impossible; to show once more to the world the power that resides in justice—this is to accomplish a noble task.

CHAPTER VII.

THE PRESENT CRISIS.

We now possess the principal elements of our solution; we can approach the problem just propounded by the present crisis, and, confining ourselves no longer to the appreciation of the past, can glance at the future. Not, indeed, that I make any pretensions to prophecy; political predictions, suspected with reason in all times, should be still more so at our epoch, which is that of the unforeseen. But I have a right to prove that the work which is being pursued in America is, as I have affirmed, a work of elevation, not of destruction. The dangers which the nation is advancing to meet are nothing, compared with those towards which it was lately progressing; the election of Mr. Lincoln, and the secession of the cotton States have introduced a new position which at last affords a glimpse of real chances of salvation.

I have named secession: what are we to think of the principle on which it rests? For this question another may be substituted: what is a Confederation? If we reduce it, which is inadmissible, to a simple league of States, it still remains none the less binding on each of them, so long as the end of the league remains intact. Never yet existed on earth, a federal compact conceived in this wise: "The States which form a part of this league will remain in it only till it pleases them to leave it." Such, notwithstanding, is the formula on which the Southern theorists make a stand. Among the anarchical doctrines that our age has seen hatched, (and they are numerous,) this seems to me worthy of occupying the place of honor. This right of separation is simply the *liberum veto* resuscitated for the benefit of federal institutions. As in the horseback diets of Poland, a single opposing vote could put a stop to every thing, so that it only remained to vote by sabre-strokes, so Confederations, recognizing the right of separation, would have no other resort than brute force, for no great nation can allow itself to be killed without defending itself.

Picture to yourselves, I intreat you, the progress that political demoralization would make under such a system. As there is never a law or a measure that is not displeasing to some one, it would be necessary to live in the presence of the continually repeated threat: "If the law passes, if the measure is adopted, if the election takes place, if you do not do all I want, if you do not yield to all my caprices, I leave you, I constitute myself an independent State, I provoke the formation of a rival Confederacy." The worst causes are the readiest to threaten in this style; having nothing reasonable to say in their own favor, they willingly proceed to violence, and the saying of Themistocles would find here a legitimate application: "You are angry, therefore, you are wrong."

What the result of this would be, we can imagine. No question would be longer judged by its own merits; the despotism of bad men would be established; expedients would take the place of principles; fear would put justice to flight; national resolutions would be nothing more than compromises and bargains. This, we must admit, is something like what has been passing in the United States since the South proclaimed its ultra policy, and placed its pretensions under the protection of its threats. If they had once more bowed the head, all would have been lost; the dignity, the mental liberty of America, would have suffered complete shipwreck; of all this noble system of government, there would have remained standing but a single maxim: Accord always and everywhere whatever is necessary to prevent the separation of the South. Unconstitutional in all places, the theory of separation is doubly so in the United States, where the federal system is more concentrated than elsewhere. It is without doubt a federal system; the separate States preserve the right in it of regulating their special legislation, of governing themselves as they choose, and even of holding and practising principles which are profoundly repugnant to other parts of the Confederation; the central power is, however, endowed with an extended sphere.

It has its taxes, its officers, its army, its courts; it possesses in the Territory of the different States federal property depending upon it alone; in fine, its general government and general legislation apply to the effective handling of all the essential interests of the nation. I am not surprised that the American Confederation is so strongly cemented together, excluding the pretended right of separation better than any other; the States that united towards the close of the last century were already in the habit of acting in concert; they were of the same blood, and had lived under the same rule;

their history, their interests, their customs, their tongue, their religion, all contributed to bind them closely to each other.

Besides, the question is unanimously resolved in the United States. Apart from the *fire-eaters*, not a person is found who has the slightest doubt as to the impossibility of modifying, by the violent decision of a few, the common Constitution which contains the enumeration of the States, and which can only be amended by a solemn act, voted in the special form prescribed by the compact. Mr. Lincoln merely expressed the general opinion when he said the other day: "The Union is a regular marriage, not a sort of free relation which can be maintained only by passion." *Secession is Revolution* is a political axiom which has been current at all times in the United States. It is because they are something else than a juxtaposition of States, that they comprise, by the side of a Senate in which all the States are equal, a House of Representatives, in which the number of deputies is in proportion to the population. "Our Constitution," wrote Madison, "is neither a centralized State nor a Federal Government, but a blending of the two." The experience which they had had from 1776 to 1789 had taught the different States the necessity of giving a more concentrated character to their federation. Let us not forget that they are bound by oath to remain faithful to *perpetual union*, and that there is not a federal officer in America who has not sworn to maintain this Union.

I shall not dwell on the fact that the Confederation purchased with its money two of the States that now pretend to secede from it; that it gave seventy-five millions to France for Louisiana, and twenty-five millions to Spain for Florida; no, I choose to appeal from this to precedents, the authority of which is not contested, and which form, in some sort, the interpreting commentary of the Constitution. In the last century, the State of New York, on giving in its adhesion to the Constitution, desired to reserve to itself this same power of seceding some day if it pleased; but such a reservation was rejected. At the epoch of the war of 1812 and the embargo laws, a convention of the New England States assembled at Hartford, and talked of eventual separation, whereupon the Southern party likened all separation without consent to treason, and this doctrine was sustained by the *Richmond Inquirer*, the organ of Jefferson. When, afterwards, South Carolina, accustomed to the fact, dared proclaim that act of nullification which was the prelude to a complete renunciation of federal obligations, it was plainly signified to her that a revolt would be suppressed by force of arms, and she yielded on the spot. When, the other day, this same South Carolina lowered the colors of the United States, and unfurled the Palmetto flag, Mr. Buchanan himself proclaimed (how could he do otherwise?) the flagrant illegality of such an act; it is true, that, after having declared it illegal, he took care to disavow all intention of putting the law in force.

And this same conduct of Mr. Buchanan is the precise explanation of the prodigious haste which the South Carolinians have used in their proceedings. They knew that the President in power could not, if he would, act with vigor against his own party. His inaction was assured; there were two months of interregnum, of which it was important to make the most; so that Mr. Lincoln, on coming into office, might find himself checked, or at least harassed, by the power of a deed accomplished.

It seems as though Mr. Buchanan was anxious himself to give the signal of revolt. The message that was issued by him, after the election of Mr. Lincoln, is really the most extraordinary document ever written by the head of a great State; he doubtless declares in it that a regular election cannot of itself alone furnish sufficient cause for the violence of the South; he takes care, however, to add that the South has reason to complain, that reparation and guarantees are due it, and that if these are refused, (that is, if the North refuses to replace its head under the yoke, and to decree at once the ruin and the shame of America,) it will then be time for action.

The Carolinians thought that they might be excused for being a little less prudent than the first magistrate of the United States, since, moreover, they saw their pretensions sanctioned by him. Why not attack the Confederation while it had a chief who was determined to make as little defence as possible? The weakness of Mr. Buchanan justified the confidence of Carolina. He refrained to place in the Federal fortresses troops destined to protect them against an expected assault; when a brave man, Major Anderson, took measures to defend the post that had been confided him, this unexpected resistance by which the programme was deranged, appeared as ill-timed to Mr. Buchanan as insolent to the people of Charleston; and the despatch of the 30th of December, addressed to their commissioners, exculpates him from the crime of having sent the reinforcements, and makes excuses in pitiful terms for the conduct of Major Anderson, whom they ought to hear before condemning. In fact, Anderson acted on his own responsibility, and incurred the blame of the Minister of War, who advised in full council the surrender of the forts.

The American Government is as timid as the seceded States are resolute. Our generation, which has witnessed sad spectacles, has never yet, perhaps, contemplated any more humiliating. Ministers, one of whom, hardly out of the Cabinet, has gone to preside over the secession convention at Montgomery, and another of whom has taken care to pave the way in advance for the revolt of the South, and to secure for it the resources of money, arms, and munitions, which it was about to need; ministers who vote openly for the insurgents, whose financial intrigues have been proved by investigation, and whose electoral manœuvres, duplicated by embezzlement of public money, have ended in a sort of political treason, disavowed only by General Cass; a Cabinet, in the last extremity, still essaying to continue its former course by killing with its veto the bill adopted by the Legislature of Nebraska to prohibit slavery in its Territory; a Government falling apart by piecemeal, for fear of compromising itself by resisting some part of the South: do you know of any thing so shameful? Mr. Buchanan will end as he began: for four years, he has been struggling to obtain an extension of slavery; for a month, he has been favoring the plans of separation, by opposing his force of inertia to the growing indignation of the North.

Being unable to prevent every thing, he does at least what he can: forced to send some reinforcements, he speedily withdraws them in a manner seemingly designed to render easy the attack on Fort Sumter and to discourage Major Anderson. In the hands of a President who understood his duties, things would have gone on very differently. In the first place, the South would have known on what to rely, and would have been reminded of the message of General Jackson in 1833, exacting the *immediate* disbanding of its troops; next, preliminary measures of precaution would not have been systematically neglected; lastly, at the first symptom of revolt, a sufficient number of ships of war would have been sent to Charleston to insure the regular collection of taxes and respect for the Federal property. Nothing is so pacific as resolution:

face to face with a strong Government, we look twice before launching into adventures; but, with Mr. Buchanan, it was almost impossible for the cotton States to refrain from precipitating themselves headlong into them. The repression that will come by and by will not repair the evil that has been done. Explanations will also follow too late; it was for the President to reply on the spot, and categorically, to the manifestos issued by the South. To let the violent States know that their unconstitutional plans would meet a prompt chastisement; to let the neighboring States know that their sovereignty was by no means menaced, and that they would continue to regulate their internal institutions as they pleased; to say to all that the discussion of plans of abolition was not in question; to say too to all that the majorities of free-soilers would be protected in the Territories, and that the conquests of slavery were ended: what language would have been better fitted than this to isolate the Gulf States—perhaps to check them?

I say *perhaps*, because I know that passions had reached such a pitch of exasperation that a rupture seemed inevitable. In South Carolina, for example, the Governor had recommended both Houses in advance to take measures for seceding if

Mr. Lincoln should be elected; a special commission was nominated, and held permanent session. In Texas, Senator Wigfall did not fear to say, in supporting Mr. Breckenridge: "If any other candidate is elected, look for stormy weather. There may be a Confederation, indeed, but it will not number more than thirty-three States." Mr. Jefferson Davis, of Mississippi, and Mr. Benjamin, of Louisiana, held no less explicit language, announcing that at the first electoral defeat of the South, it would set about forming a separate Confederation, long since demanded by its true interests.

What the South called its "interests," what it ended by adopting as a political platform, outside of which there was no safety, was, as we have seen, the subjugation of majorities in the Territories, the restriction of sovereignty in the Northern States, the reform of the liberty bills, which refused the prisons of these States and the co-operation of their officers, to the Federal agents charged with arresting fugitive slaves, the power of transporting slavery over the whole Confederation, the duty of extending indefinitely the domain of slavery. Who paid Walker? Who continually recruited bands of adventurers to launch on Cuba or Central America? Who prepared the well-known lists of slave

States with which the South counted on enriching itself: four States some day to be carved out of Texas, (the South had caused this to be authorized in advance,) three States to be created in the Island of Cuba, an indefinite number of States to be detached one after another from Central America and Mexico? Who clamorously demanded the reëstablishment of the African slave trade, alone capable of peopling this vast extent, and of lowering the excessive price of the negroes supplied by the producing States? The extreme South, which alone was concerned in this, saw gigantic vistas opening before it on which it fastened with ecstasy. Now, already, in spite of the more or less avowed support of Mr. Buchanan, its success was already checked, it felt itself provoked and thwarted. Henceforth, all its hopes were concentrated on the election of 1860: we may judge, therefore, of its disappointment, and of the furious ardor with which it must have seized upon its last resource, namely, secession, which might prove in its hands either a means of terrifying the North, and of bringing it again under the yoke, or of entering alone into a new destiny, of having elbow-room, and of devoting itself entirely to the propagation of slavery!

The facts are known; I do not think of recounting them. I content myself with remarking the enthusiasm which prevails in the majority of the cotton States. One could not commit suicide with a better grace. It is easy to recognize a country hermetically sealed to contradiction, which is enchanted with itself, and which ends by accomplishing the most horrible deeds with a sort of conscientious rejoicing. The enthusiasm which is displayed in proclaiming secession, or in firing on the American flag, is displayed in freeing the captain of a slaver, a noble martyr to the popular cause. There is something terrifying in the enthusiasm of evil passions. When I consider the folly of the South, which so heedlessly touches the match to the first cannon pointed against its confederates; when I see it without hesitation give the signal for a war in which it runs the risk of perishing; when I read its laws, decreeing the penalty of death against any one who shall attack the Palmetto State, and its dispatches, in which the removal of Major Anderson is exacted, in the tone which a master employs toward a disobedient servant, I ask myself whether the present crisis could really have been evaded, and whether any thing less than a rude lesson could have opened eyes so obstinately closed to the light.

People have taken in earnest the plans of the

Southern Confederacy. Nothing could be more imposing, in fact, if they had the least chance of success. The fifteen Southern States, already immense, joined to Mexico, Cuba, and Central America—what a power this would be! And, doubtless, this power would not stop at the Isthmus of Panama: it would be no more difficult to reëstablish slavery in Bolivia, on the Equator, and in Peru, than in Mexico. Thus the "patriarchal institution" would advance to rejoin Brazil, and the dismayed eye would not find a single free spot upon which to rest between Delaware Bay and the banks of the Uruguay. Furthermore, this colossal negro jail would be stocked by a no less colossal slave trade: barracoons would be refilled in Africa, slave expeditions would be organized on a scale hitherto unknown, and whole squadrons of slave ships (those "floating hells") would transport their cargoes under the Southern colors, proudly unfurled; patriotic indignation would be aroused at the mere name of the right of search, and the whole world would be challenged to defend the liberty of the seas.

Such is the project in its majestic unity. Such is the glorious ideal which the extreme South hoped to attain by its union with the North, and which it now seeks to attain by its separation. The hearts of men beat high at the thought, and many are ready to give their lives heroically in order to secure its realization. Alas! we are thus made; passion excuses every thing, transfigures every thing.

Each one feels instinctively, moreover, that no part of the plan can be separated from the whole; that it must be great to be respected; that to people this vast extent with slaves, the African slave trade is indispensable; of course, they took care not to avow all this at the first moment; it was necessary, in the beginning, to delude others, and perhaps themselves; it was necessary to obtain recognition. On this account, the prudent politicians who have just drawn up the programme of the South, have been careful to record in it the prohibition of the African slave trade, and the disavowal of plans of conquest. But this does not prevent the necessities of the position from becoming known by and by. True programmes, adapted to the position of affairs, are not changed from day to day. I defy the slave States, provided their Confederation succeeds in existing, to do otherwise than seek to extend towards the South; hemmed in on all sides by liberty, incessantly provoked by the impossibility of preventing the flight of their negroes, they will fall on those of their neighbors who are the least capable of resistance, and whose territory is most to their convenience. This fact is obvious, as it is also obvious that they will have recourse to the African slave trade to people these new possessions. It is in vain to deny it, on account of Europe, or of the border States; the necessities will subsist, and, sooner or later, they will be obeyed. If the border States persist in deluding themselves on this point, and fancy that they will always keep the monopoly of this infamous supply of negroes sold at enormous prices, this concerns them. In any case, the illusion will finally become dispelled. It is not in the nomination of Jefferson Davis as President of the Confederate States, that we are to look for the final repudiation of those projects of which this politic man is in some sort the living representative.

And when they are renewed, we shall see an invincible obstacle rise up in the way of the realization of a plan so monstrous. As soon as the African slave trade is established, the domestic slave trade will cease, the revenues of the producing States will be suppressed, the price of negroes will fall everywhere, and the fortunes of all the planters will fall in like proportion. Can it be possible that they will accept the chances of civil war, of insurrections, and of massacres, in order to ensure to themselves the risk of ruin in case of success? Can it be possible, above all, that Europe will lend a hand, as we seem to imagine, to the most audacious attack ever directed against Christian civilization?

I know that we must always make allowance for probable perfidy, and I am far from dreaming, as times go, that chivalric Europe will refuse to serve her own interests because these interests would cost her principles something. No, indeed, I imagine nothing of the sort; yet I think that I should wrong the nineteenth century if I supposed it capable of certain things. There are sentiments which cannot be provoked beyond measure with impunity.

Remember the shudder that ran through the world when Texas, a free country, was transformed into slave territory as the result of the victory of the United States; multiply the crime of Texas by ten, by twenty, and you will have a faint image of the impression of disgust that the Southern republic is about to call forth among us.

It is important that they should know this in advance at Charleston, and not delude themselves as to the kind of welcome for which the Palmetto State and its accomplices have to hope. Not only will no one recognize their pretended independence at this time, for to recognize it would be to tread under foot the evident rights of the United States, but they will excite one of those moral repulsions which the least scrupulous policy is forced to take into account. It is one thing to hold slaves; it is another to be founded expressly to serve the cause of slavery on earth; this is a new fact in the history of mankind. If a Southern Confederacy should ever take rank among nations, it will represent slavery, and nothing else. I am wrong; it will also represent the African slave trade, and the fillibustering system. In any case, the Southern Confederacy will be so far identified with slavery, with its progress, with the measures designed to propagate and perpetuate it here below, that a chain and whip seem the only devices to be embroidered on its flag.

Will this flag cover the human merchandise which it is designed to protect against the interference of cruisers? Will there be a country, will there be a heart, forgetful enough of its dignity to tolerate this insolent challenge flung at our best sympathies? I doubt it, and I counsel the Carolinians to doubt it also. The representative of England at Washington is said to have already declared that in presence of the slave trade thus practised, his government will not hesitate to pursue slavers into the very ports of the South. France will hold no less firm a tone; whatever may be the dissent as to the right of search, the *right of slave ships*, be sure, will be admitted by none; a sea-police will soon be found to put an end to them; if need be, the punishment will be inflicted on their crews that is in store for a much less crime, that of piracy; these wretches will be hung with short shrift at the yard-arm, without form or figure of law.

The Carolinians deceive themselves strangely. They fancy that they will be treated with consideration, that they will even be protected, because they maintain the principle of free trade, and because they hold the great cotton market. Free trade, cotton, these are the two recommendations upon which they count to gain a welcome in Europe. Let us see what we are to think of this.

I shall not be suspected in what I am about to say of free trade—I, who have always been its declared partisan; I, who sustained it twenty years ago as candidate in the bosom of one of the electoral colleges of Paris, and who applauded unreservedly our recent commercial treaty with England; but man does not live by bread alone, and if ever a school of commercial liberty should anywhere be found that should carry the adoration of its principle so far as to sacrifice to it other and nobler liberties, a school disposed to set the question of cheapness above that of justice, and to extend a hand to whoever should offer it a channel of exportation, maledictions enough would not be found for it. Let England take care; those who have no love for her, take delight in foretelling that her sympathies will be weighed in the balance with her interests, and that the protection of the North risks offending her much more than the slavery of the South. I am convinced that it will amount to nothing, and that we shall once more see how great is the influence of Christian sentiment among Englishmen. Should the reverse be true, we must veil our faces, and give over this vile bargaining, adorned with the name of free trade, to the full severity of public opinion.

I repeat that it will amount to nothing. Moreover, do not let us exaggerate either the protective instincts of the North or the free trade of the South. The new tariff just adopted at Washington (a grave error, assuredly, which I do not seek to palliate) may be amended in such a manner as to lose the character of prohibition with which certain States have sought to invest it. Let us not forget, that by the side of Pennsylvania, which urges the excessive increase of taxes, the North counts a considerable number of agricultural States, the interests of which are very different. Now, these are the States which elected Mr. Lincoln, and which will henceforth have the most decisive weight on the destinies of the Union. We may be tranquil, the protective reaction which has just triumphed in part will not long be victorious. All liberties cling together: the liberty of commerce will have its day in the United States.

But if all liberties cling together, all slaveries cling together also, and cannot be liberal at will, even in commercial matters. The Southern States plume themselves on being thus liberal, and it is sought to give them this reputation. However, the facts are little in harmony with their brilliant programme. Far from proclaiming free trade, the "Confederate" States, by a formal act adopted on the 18th of February, have maintained the tariff of 1857. They have gone further: their Congress has just established a new and relatively heavy tax, which must burden the exportation of cotton. This is not commercial liberty as I understand it.

Notwithstanding, the watchword has been given, the champions of slavery have skilfully organized their system of manœuvre in Europe, and it is developing according to their wishes. To be indignant at the new tariff, to speak only of the new tariff, to create by means of the new tariff a sort of popularity for the Southern republic—such is the end which they sought to attain. I doubt whether they have fully obtained it, although the South, I say it to our shame, has already succeeded in procuring friends and praisers among us. The factitious indignation will fall without doubt; but cotton remains: at the bottom, the South counts much more upon cotton than free trade to bring the Old World into her interests. On rushing into a mad enterprise, all the perils of which, enraged as it was, it could not disguise, it said to itself that its cotton would protect it. Is it not the principal and almost the only producer of a raw material, without which the manufactures of the whole world would stand still? Are there not millions of workmen in England (one-sixth of the whole population!) who live by the manufacture of cotton? Is not the wealth of Great Britain founded on cotton, which alone furnishes four-fifths of its exported manufactures? All this is true, and they are not ignorant of it at Manchester. Notwithstanding, what happened there the other day? An immense meeting was convoked for the purpose of carefully examining the great cotton business, and the perils created by the present crisis. I do not know that among these manufacturers, knowing that their interests were menaced, that among these workmen, knowing that their means of livelihood were at stake, that from the heart of this country, knowing that want, famine, and insurrections might come to her door, there arose a voice, a single one, to address a word of sympathy to the Southern States, and to promise them the slightest support. It was because there was something transcending manufacturing supplies, and even the bread of families: the need, I am glad to state, of protesting against certain crimes. Instead of extending a hand to the secessionists of Charleston, the English manufacturers resolutely laid the foundation of a vast society, destined to develop on the spot the production of cotton by free labor in India, the Antilles, and Africa. Such was their answer; and if you knew their most secret thoughts, you would have no difficulty in discovering that the ambition of the South, its turbulent policy, and its aggressions without pretext, are far from exciting the gratitude of English commerce, or of inspiring its confidence.

Every one in England comprehends that, from the standpoint of interest, the separation of the

South is a mortal blow dealt to the cotton production, which will henceforth have the aid neither of credit nor entrepôts, and which is advancing towards catastrophes which may involve a conflict of arms. From another and higher standpoint, the public opinion of England has not made us wait for its verdict: already its abolition societies have regained life and begun their movements; already, under the pressure of the universal feeling, the Court of Queen's Bench has revised the affair of the negro Anderson, to deliver into the strong hands of the metropolis a question before which the judicial authority of Canada hesitated, and to pronounce at length a verdict of acquittal.

The South has taken account in its calculations neither of man nor God. God especially seems to have been forgotten, though it placed itself formally under his protection. Who does not shudder at the enunciation of these unheard-of plans: we will do this, then we will do that; we will hold England through cotton, we will entice France through influence—we will have many negroes, much produce, and much money! And what will God think of it? Everywhere else but in South Carolina, this question would appear formidable beyond expression.

If the South has taken its wishes for realities in Europe, it has committed the same error in America. Its secession has some chance (and what a chance!) only on condition of drawing in all the slave States without exception; now it seems by no means probable that such a unanimity, supposing it to be gained by surprise, could ever be maintained successfully. The negro-raising States could not possibly regard the future in the same light as the consuming States. Their revenues are based on the value of the domestic slave trade, which bears no resemblance to that of the African slave trade. Ask Virginia or Maryland long to sustain a policy, the result of which would be to lower the price of her slaves in one day from a thousand dollars to two cents! This is so clearly felt in the extreme South, that the provisional constitution, adopted at Montgomery, is drawn up with an express view to reassuring the producing States on this point. They are afraid of the African slave trade! It shall not be reopened. They are anxious to sell their negroes! They shall be bought only of those States forming part of the Southern Confederacy. It belongs to them to ask now whether this Montgomery constitution, adopted for a year, really guarantees any thing to them, and whether it is possible that an attempt will not be made to revive the African slave trade, provided the Southern Confederacy succeeds in enduring. However this may be, they are held apart by so many causes, that they would only unite to-day to separate to-morrow. I know well that the passions of slavery rule in many of the border States, especially in Virginia, as violently as in the extreme South. I do not disguise from myself that the habit of sustaining a deplorable cause in common has created between the border and the cotton States a bond of long standing and difficult to break. But I say this: the impulses of the first hour will have their morrow; when the frontier States witness the commencement of those territorial invasions which must necessarily bring the African slave trade in their train; when they know what reliance to place on the fine promises made to-day to attract them; when they perceive that in separating from the North, they themselves have removed the sole obstacle in the way of the flight of all their slaves; when, in fine, they feel weighing upon them, and them first, the perils of an armed struggle and a negro insurrection, they will listen perhaps to those of their citizens who, even now, are urging them to turn to the side of justice—of justice and of safety.

By the fewness of their slaves, by the nature of their climate, which resembles that of Marseilles and Montpellier, by the kind of cultivation to which their country is adapted, by the number of manufactures which are beginning to be established among them, it seems as if they must be led, or, at least, some day led back, to the policy of union. This is no discovery: the *seceded States* know it already; they form a separate band. America has not forgotten the retreat of the seven, which, a few months ago, dismembered the Democratic Convention assembled at Charleston. These seven were South Carolina, Florida, Alabama, Mississippi, Arkansas, Texas, and Louisiana; in other words, all those States which were the first to vote for secession. The same list, with the addition of Georgia and North Carolina, appeared again on the day of the Presidential election: these nine States alone adopted Mr. Breckenridge as their candidate.

Here, then, is a profound distinction, which attaches to interests and tendencies, which has manifested itself already, which will manifest itself more and more, and which will work, sooner or later, the salvation of the United States. The border States cannot unite with the cotton States definitively. They gave proofs of this in the last election. Five among them, Tennessee, Kentucky, Delaware, Virginia, and Maryland, at that time took an intermediate position by making an intermediate choice: Mr. Bell. Without going so far, Missouri protested at least against the nomination of Mr. Breckenridge by casting its vote for Mr. Douglas. Better than this, a declared adversary of slavery, Mr. Blair, was elected representative by this same slave State, Missouri, on the day before the balloting for the presidency; and on the next day his friends voted openly for Mr. Lincoln, while no one dared annul their votes, as had been done four years before. Mr. Lincoln thus obtained fifteen thousand votes in Missouri, four thousand in Delaware, fifteen hundred in Maryland, a thousand in Kentucky, and as many in Virginia. The figures are nothing; the symptom is significant. The slave States of this intermediate region contain in their bosom, therefore, men who do not fear to attack the "patriarchal institution." Have we not just seen a Republican committee acting at Baltimore, in the midst of Maryland? Has not this same Maryland just rejected, by the popular vote, the infamous law which its legislature had adopted, and by virtue of which free negroes who should not quit the State would be reduced by right to slavery? When I remember these facts, so important and so recent, I comprehend how it is that a Kentuckian holds the South at bay behind the menaced walls of Fort Sumter, and how the cabinet of Mr. Lincoln has ministers in its midst, who belong to the border States.

People take the peculiar situation of the border States too little into account in looking into the future which is preparing for America. They persist in presenting to us two great confederacies, and, in some sort, two United States, called to divide the continent. If any thing like this could occur, it could not endure. Doubtless, there are hours of vertigo from which we may look for every thing, even the impossible; and, who knows? perhaps the impossible most of all; nevertheless, the border States cannot attach themselves forever to a cause which is not their own. By the side of the manifestations which have taken place in Virginia and South Carolina, we have already a right to cite demonstrations of a different kind. Has not Missouri just decided prudently, that, in the matter of separation, the decisions of her legislature shall not be valid until ratified by the whole people? This little resembles the eagerness with which States elsewhere rush into secession. It is therefore probable that the United States will keep or soon bring back into their bosom a considerable number of the border States. By their side, the gulf States will attempt to form a rival nation, aspiring to grow towards the South. Such is the true extent of the separation that is preparing.

Suppose these projects to become, some day, realities, we may ask whether a real weakening of the United States would be the result. Suppose even that another secession, based on different motives, which nothing foretells at present, should take place beyond the Rocky Mountains; suppose that a Pacific republic should some day be founded, would the American Confederation have reason to be greatly troubled at witnessing the formation on her sides of the association of the gulf States, California, and Oregon? Look at a map, and you will see that the valley of the Mississippi, and of the lakes, and the shores of the Atlantic, are not necessarily connected either with the Gulf of Mexico, (save the indispensable outlet at New Orleans,) or the regions beyond the great desert and the Rocky Mountains, the land of the Mormons and the gold-diggers. Unity is not always the absolute good, and it may be that progress must come through disruption. Who knows whether instantaneous secession would not perform the mission of resolving certain problems otherwise insoluble? Who knows whether slavery must not disappear in this wise in the very effort that it makes to strengthen itself through isolation? Who knows whether it is not important to the prosperity and real power of the United States to escape from theories of territorial monopoly, those evil counsellors but too much heeded? Who knows, in fine, whether the day will not come, when, the questions of slavery once settled, new federal ties will again bind to the centre the parts that stray from it to-day?

I put these questions; I make no pretensions to resolve them. In any case, the imagination has had full scope for some time past. People have not been satisfied with the Southern Confederacy; have they not invented both the pretended Pacific Confederacy which I have just mentioned, and the central Confederacy, in which the border States will take shelter in common with two or three free States, as Pennsylvania and Indiana? Have they not supposed, in the bargain, (for they seem to find it necessary to discover the dissolution of the Union everywhere at all costs,) that the agricultural population of the West, discontented with the tariff recently adopted, and putting in practice the new maxim, according to which they are to have recourse to separation, instead of pursuing reforms, will seek an asylum in Canada? I need not discuss such fables. I am convinced, for my part, that the principle of American unity is much more solid than people affirm; I see in the United States a single race, and almost a single family: they may divide, they will not cease to be related. The relationship will take back its rights. For the time, however, secession seems to have a providential part to enact. It facilitates, in certain respects, the first steps of Mr. Lincoln; thanks to it, the hostile majority in the Senate is blotted out, the uncertainty of the House of Representatives is decided, the Government becomes possible. In the face of the senators and representatives of the gulf States, I do not see how Mr. Lincoln could have succeeded in acting. Did not the Senate, last year, adopt the proposition of Mr. Jefferson Davis in opposition to the liberty of the Territories? Congress would have trammelled, one after another, all the measures of the new administration. Now, on the contrary, the rôle of the victorious party will be easy; its preponderance is assured in both Houses; the Supreme Court will cease, ere long, to represent the doctrines of the extreme South, and to issue Dred Scott decrees. This is a vast change. General Cass, in truth, comprehended the interests of slavery better than Mr. Buchanan, when he demanded that the Government should arrest with vigor from the beginning the faintest wish of separation.

CHAPTER VIII.

PROBABLE CONSEQUENCES OF THE CRISIS.

General Cass was nearer right than he himself imagined. In arresting from the beginning the development of the plans of the South, by a vigorous attitude, and by the blockade, then easy, of Charleston, the Government would not only have rendered it the trifling service of maintaining its means of opposition in Congress, but also the inappreciable boon of averting the dangers of war. What has happened, on the contrary? Precisely what must have happened, the human heart being such as it is. When on one side is found all the ardor, all the activity, all the resolution, and, into the bargain, all the apparent success, while on the other is found languor, hesitation, inaction, and disgraceful delays, it happens almost infallibly that the undecided are hurried away by the fanatics.

Let the United States take care! the chances of

the future incur the risk, at this moment, of becoming more grave. To-day, the border States are on the point of declaring themselves; to-day, in consequence, it is important to offer to their natural irresolution the support of a policy as firm as moderate. Given over without defence to the ardent solicitations of the extreme South, they are only too likely to yield, particularly if the Federal Government give them reason to believe that the separation will encounter no serious obstacle.

We must remember that ignorant communities are here in question, who are ruled by their prejudices, and who have never tolerated the slightest show of discussion upon questions connected with the subject of slavery. Such communities are capable of committing the most egregious follies; panics, sudden resolutions, mistaken unanimities, are common among them. Formerly, kings were pitied who lived surrounded by flatterers, it was said (we have provided against that) that the truth never reached them; the planters are the only men I see to-day that can be likened to these monarchs of olden time; neither books, nor journals, nor preachers, are permitted to point out to them their duties or their interests in the matter of slavery.

The slightest symptom of inertia or of feebleness in the Federal Government at this time, will, therefore, expose the border States to great perils, and, through them, the whole Confederation. As easy as it would have been, with a little energy, to prevent the evil, to confine secession within its natural limits, and to weaken the chances of civil war, so difficult has it become, at present, to attain the same end. Painful duties, perhaps, will be imposed on Mr. Lincoln. I wonder, in truth, at the politicians who advise him to a "masterly inactivity," that is, who urge him to continue Mr. Buchanan! Doubtless he does right to leave to the insurgents all the odium of acting on the offensive, but his moderation should detract nothing from his firmness, and it is even of importance that the means of action which he is about to prepare, should manifest so clearly the overwhelming superiority of the North, that the resistance of the South will be thereby discouraged.

Adversaries of slavery are not wanting, who are almost indignant at the adoption of such measures by the new President. Did they fancy then that a formidable question could be resolved without risking the repression of the assaults of force by force? Away with childishness! In electing Mr. Lincoln, it was known that the cotton States were ready to protest with arms in their hands; he was not elected to receive orders from the cotton States, or to sign the dissolution of the United States on the first requisition. Who wills the end, wills the means. No one, certainly, desires, more than myself, the peaceful repression of the rebellion. May the success of the blockade render the employment of the army useless! May the resolute attitude of the Confederation arrest the majority of the intermediate States on the dangerous declivity upon which they are standing! Once let them be drawn into the circle of influence of the extreme South, and little chance will remain of confining the civil war within the limits beyond which it is so important that it should not spread.

Then will appear the *irrepressible conflict* of Mr. Seward. Whether desired or not, if the two Confederations are placed side by side, the one representing all the slavery, the other representing all the liberty, the conflict will take place. It will take place perhaps now, perhaps a little later; however this may be, no one will have the power to hinder it. Suppose the South, thus completed, relinquish (and nothing is less certain) the opening by itself of a war in which it must perish, and its great plans of attack, against Washington, for instance, be abandoned; suppose the United States, on their side, avoid a direct attack, which might give the signal for insurrections; suppose they limit themselves to purely maritime repression of the revolt; that, after striking off the Southern harbors from the list of seaports, and declaring that custom-house duties cannot be legally paid there, they maintain this blockade, which Europe ought to applaud; would they have averted all chances of conflict? No; alas! However temporary such a situation might be, complaints, recriminations, and, ere long, violent reprisals, would be seen everywhere arising. Rivalries of principles, rivalries of interests, bitter memories of past injuries, such are the rocks on which peaceful policy would be in continual danger of shipwreck.

We must not cherish illusions; the chances of civil war have been increasing for a few weeks past with fearful rapidity. If Mr. Lincoln has confined himself scrupulously to conservative and defensive measures, there has been, on the contrary, in the actions of the South, a violent precipitation which has surpassed all expectancy. It is the haste of skilful men, who attempt by a bold stroke to carry off the advantages of a deed accomplished; it is at the same time, and chiefly, perhaps, the haste of men who have nothing to lose, the ringleaders of the present hour. At the end of resources, the insurgent South has already increased its taxes inordinately; it has killed public and private credit; it has created a disturbed revolutionary condition, intolerable in the end, which no longer permits deliberation, or even reflection. Will the South pause on such a road? It is difficult to hope it. As to the North, its plan of action is very simple, and easily maintained: suppose even that through impossibility it should give over forcing the rebels back to their duty, who can ever imagine that it would suffer itself to be deprived of the mouths of the Mississippi, or that it would abandon to the rival Confederacy the capital itself of the Union, inclosed within the slave States? Let us see things as they are: the maintenance and development of slavery in the South will render the abolitionist proceedings of its neighbor intolerable in its eyes; if it has not been able to endure a contradiction accompanied with infinite circumspection, and tempered by many prudent disclaimers, how will it support this daily torture, a unanimous and well-founded censure, a perpetual denunciation of the infamies which accompany and constitute the "patriarchal institution"?

The North, on its side, will be unable to forget that, by the act of the South, without reason or pretext, the glorious unity of the nation has been broken; that the star-spangled banner has been rent in twain; that the commercial prosperity of America has been shaken at the same time with its greatness. Let one of those incidents then occur, that are constantly arising, a Southern slave ship stopped on the high seas by the North, a negotiation of the South threatening to introduce Europe into the affairs of the New World, and directly hostilities will break out.

What they will be in the end, I scarcely dare imagine. If the planters are forced, at present, to mount guard day and night, to prevent the insurrectionary movements that are constantly ready to break out on their estates; if many families are already sending their women and children into safer countries; what will it be when the arrival of the forces of the North shall announce to the slaves that the hour of deliverance has sounded? It will be in vain to deny it; their arrival will always signify this in the sight of the South. There are certain facts, the popular interpretation of which ends by being the true interpretation. I have no doubt that the generals of the United States, before attacking the Southern

Confederacy, will recommend to the negroes to remain at peace, and will disavow and condemn acts of violence; but what is a manifesto against the reality of things and the necessity of situations? There is a word that I see written in large letters everywhere in the projects of the South—yes, the word *catastrophe* is to be read there in every line. The first successes of the South are a catastrophe; the greatness of the South will be a catastrophe; and, if the South ever realize in part the iniquitous hopes towards which it is rushing, the catastrophe will acquire unheard-of proportions; it will be a St. Domingo carried to the tenth power.

One cannot, with impunity, give full scope to his imagination, and, in the year of our Lord 1861, set to work to contrive the plan of a Confederacy designed to protect and to propagate slavery. These things will be avenged sooner or later. Ah! if the South knew how important it is that it should not succeed, if it comprehended that the North has been hitherto its great, its only guarantee! This is literally true; a slave country, above all, to-day, needs to be backed up by a free country to ensure the subsistence of an institution contrary to nature; otherwise the first accident, the first war, gives it over to perils that make us shudder. Thanks to their metropolises, our colonies were able first to keep, and afterwards to enfranchise their slaves, without succumbing to the task. But let a Southern Confederacy come, in which the immigration of the whites will be naught, while the increase of the blacks will be pursued in all ways, and, in case of success, the moment will soon arrive when many States will see themselves placed, as is the case already with South Carolina, in presence of a number of slaves exceeding that of free men. Such a social monstrosity never existed under the sun; even in Greece, even in Rome, even among the Mussulmans, the total number of free men remained superior; the colonies alone, through the effect of the slave trade, presented an inverse phenomenon, and the colonies were consolidated with their metropolises in the same manner that the States of the South are consolidated with those of the North.

In this will be found, I repeat, a most important guarantee. The South in rejecting it, and imagining itself able alone to maintain a situation which will become graver day by day, deludes itself most strangely. At the hour of peril, when servile insurrection perhaps shall ravage its territory, it will be astonished to find itself left alone in the presence of its enemy.

And this enemy is not one that can be conquered once for all. Even after the victory, even in times of peace, the threat of servile insurrection will ever remain suspended over the head of the Southern Confederacy ; it will be necessary always to watch, always to be on the guard, always to repress, and, to tell the truth, always to tremble. The planters, whether they know it or not, are not preparing to sleep on a bed of roses. To labor to accomplish an iniquitous work amidst the maledictions of the universe, to increase their estates and their slaves under penalty of death, and to feel instinctively that they will die for having increased them, to tremble because of European hostility, to tremble because of American hostility, to tremble because of hostility from without and within—what a life ! That one might accept it in the service of a noble cause, I can comprehend ; but the cause of the South ! In truth, this would be taking great pains for small wages.

The South inspires me with profound compassion. We have told it, much too often, that its Confederacy was easy to found. To found, yes ; to make lasting, no. Here, it is not the first step that costs—it is the second, it is the third. The Southern Confederacy is not viable. Let us suppose that, to its misfortune, it has succeeded in all that it has just undertaken: Charleston is free, the border States are drawn in, there is a new federal compact and a new President, the Northern States have of necessity abandoned the suppression of the insurrection by force, Europe has surmounted its repugnance and received the envoys of the great Slave republic. All questions seem resolved; but no, not a single one has attained its solution.

The policy of the South must have its application. Its first article, whether it declares it or not, exacts conquests, the absorption of Mexico, for example. The fillibusters of Walker are still ready to set out, and the first moment past, when the question is to appear discreet, it is scarcely probable that they will meet with much restraint, now that the prudence of the North is no longer at hand to counterbalance the passions of Slavery.

Admit that this enterprise bring no difficult complications. For these new territories, the question will be to procure negroes. The second article of the Southern policy will find then *nolens volens*, its inevitable application: the African slave trade will be re-established. The richest planter of Georgia, Mr. Goulden, has taken care to set forth its necessity; mark the language which he held lately: "You have hardly negroes enough for the existing States; obtain the opening of the slave trade, then you can undertake to increase the number of slave States."

Will the official re-opening of the slave trade be some day effected without bringing on a storm which will destroy the new Confederacy? I cannot say. In any case, I know one thing: that the value of the slaves, and consequently that of Southern property, will experience a decline greatly exceeding that by which it is now threatened, as it is said, by the abolition tendencies of the North. Already, through the mere fact of secession, the price of negroes has diminished one-half; and more than one intelligent planter foresees the time when this price shall have diminished three-fourths, perhaps nine-tenths. Southern fortunes are falling off, therefore, with extreme rapidity, and this arises not only from the anticipated effects of the slave trade, but also from the certainty of being unable henceforth to put a stop to the escape of the slaves. These escapes, taken all in all, remained insignificant, so long as the Union was maintained; there are not more than fifty thousand free negroes in Canada. But henceforth the Southern Confederacy will have a Canada everywhere on its frontiers. How retain that slavery that will escape simultaneously on the North and the South? The Southern republic will be as it were the common enemy, and no one assuredly will aid it to keep its slaves.

It must not be believed, moreover, that it will succeed long in preserving itself from intestine divisions—divisions among the whites. If, at the first moment, when every thing is easy, unanimity is far from appearing as complete as had been foretold, it will, later, be much worse. We shall then perceive how prophetic, if I may dare say so, were the often-quoted words of Washington's farewell address: "It is necessary that you should accustom yourselves to regard the Union as the palladium of your happiness and your security; that you should watch over it with a jealous eye; that you should impose silence on any who shall ever dare counsel you to renounce it; that you should give vent to all your indignation on the first effort that shall be attempted to detach from the whole any part of the Confederation."

A very different voice, that of Jefferson, spoke the same language. A Southern man, addressing himself to the South, which talked already of seceding, he described in thrilling words the inevitable consequences of such an act: "If, to rid ourselves of the present supremacy of Massachusetts and Connecticut, we were to break up the Union, would the trouble stop there? . . . We should soon see a Pennsylvanian party and a Virginian party forming in what remained of the Confederation, and the same party spirit would agitate public opinion. By what new weapons would these parties be armed, if they had power to threaten each other continually with joining their Northern neighbors, in case things did not go on in such or such a manner! If we were to reduce our Union to North Carolina and Virginia, the conflict would break out again directly between the representatives of these two States; we should end by being reduced to simple unities."

Is not this the anticipated history of what is about to happen in the Southern Confederacy, supposing it to succeed in uniting with a part of the border States? The opening programme will last as long as programmes usually do. When the true plan of the South, veiled for a moment, shall reappear, (and it must indeed reappear, unless it perishes before it has begun to exist;) when the question shall be to increase and be peopled, to make conquests and to reëstablish the African slave trade; when the serious purpose, in a word, shall have replaced the purpose of circumstance, what will take place between the border States and the cotton States? The profound distinction which exists between them will then manifest itself, even if it does not break forth before. A new South and a new North will be formed, as hostile perhaps as the old, and less forgiving towards each other of their mutual faults, inasmuch as they will be embittered by misfortune. Nothing divides people like a bad cause that turns out badly. They think themselves united, they call themselves united, until the moment when they discover that they have neither the same end nor the same mind. I do not see why the victory of Mr. Lincoln will have transformed the South, and suppressed the divergencies which separated it into two groups: that of the Gulf States voting for Mr. Breckenridge, that of the border States voting for Mr. Douglas or Mr. Bell, and even casting ballots for Mr. Lincoln.

Not only will the Gulf States, the only true secessionists, never act in concert with the border States, but they will not be long in seeing parties spring up in their own bosom, which will be little disposed to come to terms. A sort of feudal question, as is well known, is near obtaining a position in the South; the *poor whites* there are two or three times as numerous as the planters. The struggle of classes may, therefore, break out as soon as the effected secession shall have banished to the second rank the struggle against the adversaries of slavery.

The impoverishment of the South will not aid in calming its intestine quarrels. European immigration, already so meagre in the slave States, (Charleston is the only large American city whose population has decreased, according to the last census,) European immigration, I say, will evidently diminish still more when the South shall have taken an independent and hostile position opposite the Northern States. Who will go then to expose himself lightly to the fearful chances which the first war with any country, American or European, may bring in its train? And credit will go the same way as immigration: to lend money to planters, whose entire property is continually menaced with destruction, is one of those hazardous operations from which commerce is accustomed to recoil. Deprived of the capital furnished it by New York, obtaining only with great difficulty a few onerous and precarious advances in Europe, the South will see itself smitten at once in all its means of production; and, after the harvest of 1860, which secures our supplies for a year, after that of 1861, which it will succeed, probably, in gathering, but which it will be more difficult to sell, it is not easy to divine how it will set to work to continue its crops. While the South produces less cotton, and we lose the habit of buying of it, the cotton culture will become acclimated elsewhere; the future will thus be destroyed like the present; final ruin will approach with hasty strides.

They tell us of a loan that the new Confederacy designs to contract! Unless it be transformed into a forced loan, I have little faith in its chance. They add that it will be only necessary to establish on exported cotton a duty of a few cents per pound, and the coffers of the South will be filled. But, in the first place, to export cotton, they must produce it—they must have money; it is almost impossible that the State should be rich when all its citizens are in distress; then the exportation itself will be exposed to some difficulties if the United States organize a blockade. And I say nothing of the bad effect that will be produced by this tax *à la Turque*—this tax on exportation in the very midst of plans of commercial freedom. Neither do I speak of the effect which this extra charge, which is termed trifling, but which is, in fact, considerable, will have on the sale of American cotton, already so defective, when compared with the average price of other cottons.

Poor country, which blind passion, and, above all, indomitable pride, precipitates into the path of crime and misery! Poor, excommunicated nation, whose touch will be dreaded, whose flag will be suspected, whose continually increasing humiliations will not even be compensated by a few meagre profits! The heart is oppressed at the thought of the clear, certain, inevitable future, which awaits so many men, less guilty than erring. Between them and the rest of the world there will be nothing longer in common; they will establish on their frontier a police over books and journals, essaying to prevent the fatal introduction of an idea of liberty: the rest of the world will have for them neither political sympathies, nor moral sympathies, nor religious sympathies.

Will they at least have the consolation of having killed the United States? Will a glorious confederation have perished by their retreat? No, a thousand times no. Even though they should succeed in drawing the border States into the Southern Confederacy, the United States, thank God! will keep their rank among nations. Where will the

United States be after secession? Where they were before; for a long time the gravitation of their power has been tending towards the Northwest. The true America is there, that of ancient traditions, and that of present reality. If any serious fears might have been conceived as to its duration, they disappeared on the day of the election of Mr. Lincoln. On that day, we all learned that the United States would subsist, and that their malady was not mortal.

Great news was this! Did you ever ask yourself how much would be missing here on earth if such a people should disappear? It lives and it will live. Look at the calm and confident air of the North, and compare it with the noisy violence of the South. The North is so sure of itself that it does not deign either to become angered, or to hasten; it even carries this last to extremes. It has the air of knowing that, in spite of the apparent successes which may mark the first efforts of the South, the final success must be elsewhere. Let the South take care! to have against it both right and might is twice as much as is needed to be beaten. The North supported Mr. Buchanan because it was awaiting Mr. Lincoln. Mr. Lincoln came, the North still has patience, but will end by falling into line, and the serious struggle will begin, in case of need.

The final issue of this struggle can scarcely be doubtful. On one side, I see a confederacy divided, impoverished, bending under the weight of a crushing social problem, seeing constantly on its horizon the menace of insurrections and of massacres, unable either to negotiate, or to draw the sword, or to resolve any of the difficulties from without, without thinking of the still more formidable difficulties from within; on the other side, I see the United States, masters of themselves, unanimous, knowing what they want, and placing at the service of a noble cause, a power which is continually increasing.

The match will not be equal. I cannot help believing, therefore, that the triumph of the North will be even much more complete than we imagine to-day. I do not know what is to happen, but this I know: the North is more populous, richer, more united; European immigration goes only to the North, European capital goes only to the North. Of what elements is the population of the South composed? The first six States that proclaimed their separation number exactly as many slaves as freemen. What a position! Is it probable indeed that this confederation contrary to nature, in which each white will be charged with guarding a black, can afford a long career? The South, divided, weakened, bearing in its side the continually bleeding wound of slavery, reduced to choose in the end between the direful plans which must destroy after having dishonored it, and the Union which consolidates its interests while thwarting its passions—is it possible that the South will not return to the Union?

Something tells me that if the Union be dissolved, it will be formed again. A lasting separation is more difficult than is imagined. Face to face with Europe, face to face with the United States, the great republic of the South would find it too difficult to live. To live at peace is impossible; to live without peace is not to be thought of. The great Southern republic must perish surely by its failure, and still more surely by its success, for this monstrous success will draw down its destruction. There is in America a necessity, as it were, of union. Unity is at the foundation, diversity is only on the surface; unity is bound up with the national life itself, with race, origin, belief, common destiny, a like degree of civilization, in a word, with profound and permanent causes; diversity proceeds from the accidents of institutions.

Looking only at the province of interests, is it easy to imagine an irremediable rupture between New York and Charleston, between the valley of the Mississippi and New Orleans? What would the valley of the Mississippi be without New Orleans, and New Orleans, isolated from the vast country of which it is the natural market? Can you fancy New York renouncing half her commerce, ceasing to be the broker of cotton, the necessary medium between the South and Europe? Can you fancy the South deprived of the intervention and credit which New York assures her? The dependence of the North and the South is reciprocal; if the South produces the cotton, it is the North which furnishes the advances, then purchases on its own account or on commission, and expedites the traffic with Europe. In the United States, every part has need of the whole; agricultural States, manufacturing States, commercial States, they form together one of the most homogeneous countries of which I know. I should be surprised if such a country were destined to become forever dismembered, and that, too, at an epoch less favorable to the dismemberment of great nations than to the absorption of small ones.

Shall I say all that I think? When Anglo-

Saxons are in question, we Latins are apt to deceive ourselves terribly; one would not risk much, perhaps, in supposing that events would take place precisely in the reverse of our hypothesis. We have loudly predicted in Europe the end of the United States, the birth and progress of a rival Confederacy, an irremediable separation: is not this a reason for supposing that there will be ultimately neither a prolonged separation, nor a rival Confederacy worthy of consideration? Free countries, especially those of the English race, have a habit of which we know little: their words are exceedingly violent, and their actions exceedingly circumspect. They make a great noise: one would say that every thing was going to destruction; but it is prudent to look at them more closely, for these countries of discussion are also countries of compromise, the victors are accustomed to terminate political crises by yielding something of their victory; in appearance, it is true, rather than in reality. Fully decided at heart, they consent willingly to appear less positive in form.

Here, I know that the extreme violence of the South renders a compromise very difficult, at least a present compromise. As it is accustomed to rule, and will be content with no less, as it knows that the North, decidedly emancipated, will not replace its head beneath the yoke, it seems resolved to incur all risks rather than renounce its fixed idea. For two months, the probabilities of compromise have been becoming constantly weaker. But if we have scarcely a right to count on them now, so far as the Gulf States are concerned, we must remember that the border States are at hand, that they are hesitating between the North and the South, and that certain concessions may be made to them, to prevent their separation.

Such is the true character of the discussions relating to compromise. Confined to these limits, they nevertheless possess a vast interest, for the party which the border States are about to choose, and that to which they will perhaps attach themselves afterwards, will have a great influence over the general course of the crisis. The point in question is no longer, doubtless, to retain Virginia, whose well-known passions impel her to the side of Charleston, but to induce the other States to take an attitude in conformity with their interests and their duties. It will not, therefore, be useless to give an account of the disposition that prevails among many Americans with respect to compromise.

What was produced by that Peace Conference, convoked with so much noise by Virginia, the ancient political State, the country of Washington, Jefferson, Madison, and Monroe? Nothing worth the trouble of mentioning. A considerable number of States refused to be present at this conference, which, had it been general, would have become transformed into a convention, and have annulled Congress, in point of fact, then in session in the same city? Its plan, accepted with great difficulty by a factitious majority, never appeared to have much chance of adoption. The point in question, above all, was to decide that, below a fixed latitude, the majority of the inhabitants of a Territory could not prohibit the introduction of slavery, (disguised, it is true, under the euphuistic expression, "involuntary servitude;") this measure was to be declared irrevocable, unless by the unanimous consent of the States. Despite the support of Mr. Buchanan, and that of the higher branches of trade in New York, seconded, as usual, by some fashionable circles of Boston, the almost unanimous public opinion of the North forbade all belief in the success of such an amendment to the Constitution, which, in accordance with the Constitution itself, could be adopted only on condition of uniting two-thirds of the votes of Congress to the affirmative votes of three-fourths of the States composing the Confederation.

Another project was put forward : all the members of Congress were to tender their resignation, and the new elections were to manifest the definitive will of the country on the question of slavery. That is, from the intense excitement of the country, were to be demanded some final elements of reaction, some means of disavowing the election of Mr. Lincoln. In either case, it would have been thus proved by an exceptional act that an election which is not ratified by the South may rightfully demand extraordinary measures. Now, there is nothing but what is customary, simple, and right, in the conduct of the North; it knows it, and will not, I think, permit such an advantage to be gained over it. To allow talking, to allow propositions, and to go its own way, this is the programme to which it is bound to remain faithful. What makes its honor makes also its strength: this is the privilege of good causes.

The North has not to seek bases for a compromise. They are all laid down, and I dare affirm, whatever may happen, that to these bases, constantly the same, it will not fail to return, provided, at least, that the era of compromises shall not be closed, and that the South shall not have succeeded in imposing on the North a decidedly abolition policy. To speak truly, it has but one declaration to make: to proclaim anew the constitutional law, by virtue of which each State sovereignly decides its own affairs, and consequently excludes all interference of Congress in the matter of slavery. Perhaps, alas! it will join, if need be, to this declaration, which it has never refused, the promise to respect to the utmost of its power, the principle of the restitution of fugitive slaves, which, unhappily, is also based upon the Constitution. But, on this point, promises are worth what they will fetch, for doubtless no one will imagine that it is easier to constrain the free States to accomplish an odious deed which is revolting to their conscience since they have verified their strength by electing Mr. Lincoln. Lastly, upon the ruling question, that of the Territories, the theory of the North evinces justice and clearness; between the ultra abolitionists, who wish Congress to interfere to close by force all the Territories to slavery, and the South, which wishes Congress to interfere to open by force all the Territories to slavery, it adopts this middle position: all the inhabitants of the Territories shall open or close them to slavery, according to their will. It is the right of the majority, recognized there as elsewhere.

I am not ignorant that Mr. Seward has gone much farther in the path of concession, and it is not absolutely impossible that these counsels of weakness may prevail. We must be prepared for any thing in this respect. Nevertheless, the President has by no means confirmed the imprudent words of his future prime minister. The language of Mr. Lincoln was remarkably clear in his inaugural speech, to go no further back, indicating on the spot the true, the great concession which, till new orders, may be made to the South: "Those who elected me placed in the platform presented for my acceptance, as a law for them and for me, the clear and explicit resolution which I am about to read to you: 'The maintenance intact of the right of the States, and especially of the right which each State possesses to regulate and exclusively control its institutions according to its own views, is essential to that balance of power, on which depend the perfection and duration of our political structure; and we denounce the invasion in contempt of the law by an armed force of the soil of any State or Territory, upon whatever pretext it may be, as the greatest of crimes.'" Mr. Lincoln adds further; "Congress has adopted an amendment to the Constitution, which, however, I have not seen, the purpose of which is to provide that the Federal Government shall never interfere in the domestic institutions of the States, including those which relate to persons held in service. In order to avoid all misunderstanding concerning what I have said, I depart from my intention of not speaking of any amendment in particular, to say that, considering this clause henceforth as a constitutional law, I have no objection that it be rendered explicit and irrevocable."

Concerning fugitive slaves, the inaugural discourse cites the text of the federal Constitution, which decides the question for the present; but he does not ignore the fact that this constitutional decision is as well executed as it can be, "the moral sense of the people lending only an imperfect support to the law."

As to the Territories, Mr. Lincoln declares clearly that the minority must submit to the majority, under penalty of falling into complete anarchy. Neither does he hesitate on the subject of the decisions of the Supreme Court; these decrees, in his eyes, are merely special decisions rendered in particular cases, and detracting nothing from the right which the Confederation possesses to regulate its institutions and its policy.

All this is very firm, without being provoking.

The limit of concessions is marked out, and a conciliatory spirit is maintained. It is above all in disclosing his line of conduct towards the rebellious States, that Mr. Lincoln happily resolves the problem of abandoning none of the rights of the Confederation, while manifesting the most pacific disposition, and leaving to others the odium of aggression. His doctrine on this point may be summed up in this wise: in the first place, the separation is unconstitutional, it should be, it will be combated, nothing on earth can bring the President to accede to the destruction of the Union; in the second place, he will not be the aggressor, he will endeavor to shun a war which exposes the South to fearful perils; in the third place, he will fulfill the duty of preserving federal property and collecting federal taxes in the South. In other terms, he will employ the means which should have been employed on the first day, and which would have then been more efficacious. He will attempt the establishment of a maritime blockade, in order to reduce the rebellion of the whites without provoking the insurrection of the negroes. Already, the vessels of war have been recalled from distant stations. Alas! I have little hope that the precautions dictated to Mr. Lincoln by prudence and humanity will bear their fruits. The South raises an army and is about to attack Fort Sumter, knowing that it will thus expose itself to a formidable retribution. Mr. Lincoln, in fact, has not left it in ignorance of this: "In your hands, my dissatisfied fellow-citizens, in yours and not mine, is found the terrible question of civil war. The Government will not attack you; you will have no conflict, if you are not the aggressors. You have not, on your part, an oath registered in heaven to destroy the Government; whilst I, on my side, am about to take the most solemn oath to maintain, to protect and defend it."

Such is the respective position. Men will agitate, are agitating already, about the new President, to take away from his thoughts and designs this resolute character which makes their force. They attempt to demonstrate to him, not only that Fort Sumter, so easy to revictual under Mr. Buchanan, has now become inaccessible to aid, and that no other course remains than to authorize its surrender; but that Fort Pickens itself should be surrendered to the South, in order to reserve every chance of reconciliation and in no degree to assume the responsibility of civil war! I hope that Mr. Lincoln will know how to resist these enfeebling influences. After having demonstrated to him that it is necessary to deliver up the forts, they will demonstrate to him that it is necessary to renounce the blockade, which is not tenable without the forts; then, who knows? they will demonstrate to him finally that it is necessary to sign some disgraceful compromise, and submit almost to the law of the rebels.

Once more, it is prudent to foresee every thing, and it is for this that I mention such things. I count, moreover, on their not being realized. In electing Mr. Lincoln, the United States decided thus: Slavery will make no more conquests. What they have decided, they will ultimately maintain, even though they should have the air of abandoning it. They have respected and they will respect the sovereignty of the States; upon this point they will give all the guarantees that may be desired, and Congress, we have seen, has already voted an amendment to the Constitution, designed to offer this basis of compromise. But they will go no further than this; the North must feel that, of all ways of terminating the present crisis, the most fatal would be the disavowal of principles and the desertion of the flag.

The compromises that promise any thing more than respect for the sovereignty of the States in the matter of slavery, promise more than they could perform; every one feels this, in the South as in the North. The policy of the South forms a whole of which nothing subsists if any thing be retrenched, and above all if the complicity of the Government ceases to be assured to it. On the day that the South accepts any compromise whatever, it will have renounced, not the maintenance doubtless, but the propagation of slavery; it will have renounced its rule. Compromises, (there will be such, perhaps, let us swear to nothing; before or after the war, with the entire South, or with a part of it,) compromises will be signed henceforth without any delusion. The South knows, marvellously well, that these compromises will bear little resemblance to those signed in former times. Those marked, by their constantly increasing pretension, the upward march of the South; these will mark the phases of its decline. How many changes which can never be retraced! No more conquests to promote slavery, no more reopening of the African slave trade, no more impunity secured to those numerous slave-ships which daily, to the knowledge and in the sight of all, for years past, have quitted the ports of the Confederation; no more chance of equalling, by the creation and population of new States, the rapid development of the North; henceforth the question is ended, the South must be resigned to it: the majority of the free States will become such that it can be contested neither in the House of Representatives, nor in the Senate, nor in the presidential election; the supremacy resides at the North, the programme of the South is rent in a thousand pieces.

Against this, all the compromises in the world can do nothing. If Mr. Lincoln is the first President opposed to slavery, Mr. Buchanan is the last President favorable to slavery; the American policy is henceforth fixed. Reflect, in fact, on what these four years of government will produce. The result is so enormous, that, unhappily, one might be tempted to say at Washington: "We will do all that is wished, provided we preserve the handling of affairs."

The power of a President is doubtless inconsiderable, but his advent is that of a party. This party is about to renew all administrations, great and small; the same majority which has elected him will modify before long the tendencies of the courts; in fine, the general affairs of the Union will be managed in a new spirit. It was advancing in one direction, it is about to move in the opposite.

Mr. Lincoln is not one to shut his eyes on filibustering attempts to strive to take Cuba for the slavery party, to permit States to be carved out of Mexico, and others to be made ready by subdividing Texas. The process which is about to be accomplished reminds me of the measures taken to combat a vast conflagration: the first thing done is to circumscribe its locality.

At the end of the four years of Mr. Lincoln's administration, the flames which threatened to devour the Union will be completely hemmed in. Considering the United States as a whole, and independently of the incidents of separation, we are justified in believing that the respective number of free and of slave States will leave no chance for the ulterior extension of a great scourge. Do we delude ourselves by thinking that the progress already begun in the border States will have been accelerated in its course, and that many of them will have freely passed over to the side of liberty? Is it certain, moreover, that the hesitation of some of the churches will have ceased, and that the influence of the Gospel, so decisive in America, will have finally placed itself entire at the service of the good cause?

Let there be a compromise or not, let the great

secession of the South be prevented or not, let civil war break forth or not, let it give or not give to the South the fleeting eclat of first successes, one fact remains settled henceforth: the United States were tottering on their base, they have regained their equilibrium; the deadly perils which they lately incurred from the plans of conquest of the South and the indefinite extension of slavery, are at length conjured down; they have no longer to ask whether, some day, the South having grown beyond measure, secession must not be effected by the North, leaving in the hands of the slaveholders the glorious name and the starry banner of the Union.

I think that I have gone over the whole series of hypotheses which offer any probability. I have been careful to adopt none of them, for I make no pretension, thank God, to read the future. It would be puerile to prognosticate what will happen, and not less puerile, perhaps, to describe it from what has happened. In the face of the accidents in different directions which are attracting public attention and filling the columns of newspapers, I have attempted to make a distinction between what may happen and what must endure. The lasting consequences of the present crisis are what I proposed to investigate faithfully. The reader knows what are my conclusions. It may be that it will end in the adoption of some blamable compromise; but whatever may be inscribed in it, the election of Mr. Lincoln has just written in the margin a note that will annul the text. The time for certain concessions is past, and the South has no more doubts of it than the North. It may be that the slave States will succeed in founding their deplorable Confederacy, but it is impossible that they should succeed in making it live; they will perceive that it is easier to adopt a compact or to elect a President, than to create, in truth, in the face of the nineteenth century, the nationality of slavery.

I have, therefore, the right to affirm that, whatever may be the appearances and incidents of the moment, one fact has been accomplished and will subsist: the United States were perishing, and are saved. Yes, whatever may be the hypothesis on which we pause, three new and decisive facts appear to our eyes: we know that the North henceforth has the mastery; we know that the perils which threaten the Union came from the South and not from the North; we know that the days of the "patriarchal institution" are numbered. Beneath these three facts, it is not difficult to perceive the uprising of a great people.

The victory of the North, the consciousness

which it has of its strength and of its fixed resolution, whatever may be the appearances to the contrary, to circumscribe an evil which was ready to overflow on every side, is the first fact; there is no need to return to it.

As to the second, Carolina and Georgia have charged themselves with bringing it to light. They have proved by their acts that abolitionism had been calumniated in accusing it of menacing the unity of the United States. The secessionist passions have shown themselves in the other camp; there, upon the mere news of a regular election, have been sacrificed unhesitatingly the greatness, and, it would seem, the very existence of the country. The proclamations from Charleston, and the shots fired on the Federal flag, have apprised us of what intelligent observers suspected already: that the States for which slavery had become a passion and almost a mission, must some day experience the need of procuring to such a cause the security of isolation.

And in acting in this wise, these States, strange to say, have themselves stated the problem of abolition. No one thought of it, it may be said; every one respected the constitutional limits of their sovereignty. They would not have it thus; they carried the question into the territory of Federal right and Federal relations; they exclaimed: "Secure the extension of slavery, and perish the United States!" If the United States had perished, there would not have been maledictions deep enough for those who had committed such a crime. The United States will not perish; but they will long remember with gratitude what they owe to the secessionists of 1860. When the hour of emancipation shall have struck, and it will strike some day, the secessionists of 1860 will not probably speak of their rights to indemnity; they have just given a quittance of it in cannon balls.

The third fact remains: Is it true that, in all the hypotheses, the cause of the negroes has just realized such progress that the ultimate issue of the contention can no longer be doubtful? This is most obvious. Let there be separation or not, slavery has just entered upon the road which leads to abolition, more or less rapid, but infallible. If there be no separation, this immense progress will be effected with more wisdom and slowness; violent means will be averted, the benevolent influence of the Gospel will pave the way for progressive and peaceful transformation by preaching, to the slaves as to the masters, more of their duties than of their rights. If there be separation, emancipation will be accomplished much more quickly and more calamitously. Servile war will break out; ultra abolitionism, to which hitherto the prudence of the North has refused all real credit, will be no longer restrained by the prudence of a people desirous of shunning bloody catastrophes; sustained by the increasing animosity which will inflame the two Confederacies against each other, it will find means of introducing into the South appeals to revolt, and will multiply expeditions like that of John Brown.

But let us leave these generalities, and examine nearer by, from the stand-point of emancipation, the four or five hypotheses which we have signalled out most plainly, and between which seem to lie the chances of the future.

I shall examine first of all the one whose realization is evidently pursued by the able men of the extreme South. The question is, after having speedily gained over the North, thanks to Mr. Buchanan, to arrive as quickly as possible at something which shall have the appearance and authority of a fact accomplished. Audacity, and again audacity; upon this point, the politic and the violent meet in unison to-day. It has seceded, it has invaded the Federal property, it has trumped up a government, it has given itself a President, it is about to have an army, it is already attempting to represent itself officially at the courts of the great powers.

By the side of audacity, prudence has played its part. It has taken good care not to unfurl its flag, it has made itself small, modest, moderate, as much so, at least, as the passions of the mob would permit; it asked nothing, in truth, but to live honestly in a corner of the globe. Who speaks, then, of conquests? Who would wish to re-establish the African slave trade on a large scale? Far from being retrogrades, the men of the South are champions of progress; witness their programme of commercial freedom! Are there no honest men to be found in the North, to restrain Mr. Lincoln, and to prevent him from oppressing them? Are there no governments in Europe that can interpose, and recommend the maintenance of peace? Is not this peace, which prevents the insurrections of negroes, and the destruction of cotton, for the interest of all? Why should there not be two Confederacies, living side by side, as good friends?

It is evident that the able party tend to this, and that the violent have allowed them to give, for the common interest, this subdued tone to the insurrectionary movement. The able party know too well what a prolonged war would be to desire it. They prepare for it in the hope, if not to avoid it entirely, at least to prevent its duration, and to obtain at once, in behalf of Southern secession, that species of security which is conferred in our times by the deed accomplished. Perhaps the United States, yielding to a sentiment which certainly has something honourable in it, will allow the Confederacy of the Gulf States to subsist, rather than crush it, which would be but too easy, by bringing upon it a war which would be accompanied by slave insurrections. Let us not be in haste to blame such a course; let us remember that the whole world is prompting in this direction, that all the counsels given to Mr. Lincoln, in the Old World as in the New, begin invariably with the words: "Strive to avoid civil war;" let us remember also that, to solve the American problem, much more time will be needed than we imagine in Europe; let us endeavor to put ourselves in the place of those who see things as they are, and who find themselves in a struggle with the difficulties.

Patience will doubtless have here its great inconveniencies; the Confederacy of the cotton States, if combated without vigor, will seem the living proof of the right of separation; it will be an asylum all prepared, in which the discontented border States can take refuge at need. Nevertheless the question is to tolerate this Confederacy, but by no means to recognize the legitimacy of the act which gave it birth; the question is to make use of a generous forbearance, to which new threats of secession will necessarily put an end. Then, is it nothing to manifest a spirit of peace fitted to touch the most prejudiced, to bind the majority of the border States to the destinies of the Union, to give evidence of the distinction which exists between them and the extreme South, to force them, in fine, to declare themselves? If they surmount the present temptation, (and they will never encounter a stronger one,) if they consent to sacrifice their immediate interests, and to renounce the traffic in slaves, which is in danger of ceasing from day to day in case they do not join the "Confederate States;" is such a resolution nothing? does it contain no guarantees for the future? We do not set foot in the right path with impunity; honorable resolves always carry us further, thank God! than we counted on going. Suppose even that the border States which refuse to unite with the South design to impose on the North certain vexatious conditions, they will be none the less turned from their former alliances, they will have none the less begun to move in a new direction. We should do wrong if we did not recognize how honorable is the conduct of several among them; in watching over their legislatures, in enacting that the vote of secession shall be submitted to the ratification of the whole people, certain frontier States seem to have already shown themselves resolved to foil the intrigues at Charleston.

The cause of emancipation takes, therefore, a very important step in advance, in the hypothesis of a Southern Confederacy reduced, or nearly so, to the Gulf States alone. Limited secession is perhaps of all combinations, the one most favorable to the suppression of slavery. Picture to yourself, in fact, what this Southern Confederacy will be. It will be an impossible, short-lived republic, the separation of which will one day cease, and which, meanwhile, will be incapable of realizing any of its favorite projects. From the first hour, the extreme South found itself brought to face a dilemma: either to draw in all the slave States, and then to await the moment favorable to the execution of its grandiloquent plans, to hasten towards its destiny, its ideal, to conquer territories, to people them with negroes, and to perish through the accomplishment of an impious work; or, to remain alone and undertake nothing, and still perish, but this time through impotence to exist. What is to be done when there is only the miserable Confederacy of some thousand whites, the owners and keepers of some hundred thousand blacks? Make conquests? They dare not. Open the slave trade? It would draw down destruction upon them.

Now, mark that, in the bosom of a Confederacy morally isolated from the entire world, receiving aid neither from immigrants nor capital, deprived, in a large part at least, of the fresh supply of negroes which it formerly drew from the North, unable even to incur the risk of imitating Spain, which buys *free* negroes from the slave-hunters of the African continent, not in a condition to stop the escapes which will take place on all her frontiers, the question of slavery will proceed necessarily towards its solution. The extreme South, strange to say, will find itself placed providentially as an obstacle between the United States and the countries of which it lately meditated the acquisition. The United States will have the advantage of being unable even to think of Cuba, or Central America, or Mexico; they will be delivered for a time from these baleful temptations, and from the States in which they met the warmest support. And, during this time, the extreme South will be forced, in some sort, to look at the problem of slavery under an aspect before unknown to it.

Later will come the shock, the postponed but inevitable conflict. Blockaded at the South, blockaded at the North, blockaded on the African side, undermined and torn by its intestine divisions, the extreme South will have to face, at one time or another, the irresistible power of the United States. Does any one imagine by chance that the latter will forever relinquish New Orleans and the Gulf of Mexico? The more they become elevated and strengthened, the more they will be led, say rather, forced, to absorb again the portions of their former domain which have attempted to exist without them.

From this time, the discussion relative to slavery will assume in the United States a simple and decided bearing. The extreme South, in quitting them, will have given them every facility; it will have endowed them with political homogeneousness and liberal majorities. By the mere effect of the departure of the senators and representatives of the extreme South, the party opposed to slavery will have acquired, at the outset, the numerical majority which it lacked in Congress; it will be in a position to ensure the passage of its bills, to form its administration, to constitute by degrees courts in every respect favorable to its principles. Next, the border States who shall not have followed the fortunes of the extreme South will find themselves bound to those of the North, associated with its interests, open to its ideas; and it is a fixed fact that several will not be long in completing the work of liberty already begun among them, and thus becoming, with their rich and extensive Territories, of the number of those fortunate States in which the suppression of slavery gives the signal for the fruitful invasion of immigrants, for agricultural progress, for wealth, and for credit. In this manner the "patriarchal institution" will disappear peaceably from the intermediate region, while it will be threatened by more terrible shocks in the tropical region.

This is a chance which is common to limited and to total secession, but which is still more unavoidable in the last. Face to face with the miserable Confederacy of the extreme South, the United States can afford to be patient; face to face with the Confederacy comprising all the slave States, (or, which means the same, face to face with two distinct Confederacies, comprising, the one the cotton States, the other the border States, yet united against the North through an old instinct of complicity,) the attitude of the United States, as every one foresees, will inevitably be more hostile. Total secession itself can be born only from a sentiment of declared hostility; it amounts to a declaration of war. Suppose that Mr. Lincoln rejects the advice of those of his cabinet who would incline to accept the fact of separation; suppose that, while treating the South with gentleness, and striving to spare it the horrors of an armed strife, he persists in protecting the rights of the Confederation, and securing to it, by a maritime blockade, the collection of taxes; suppose that the blockade is organized from South Carolina to the Rio Grande, supported by Forts Pickens, Jefferson, and Taylor, which will have been revictualled at all costs after the forced evacuation of Fort Sumter; suppose that, in this manner, watch is kept over the ports of Charleston, Savannah, Mobile, and New Orleans, may it not happen that the insurrectional government at Montgomery will decide to effect a march on Washington? Is it not probable that North Carolina, Virginia, and Maryland will allow themselves to be crossed without saying a word? More than this, are we not justified in believing that these States, and with them a considerable number of the central ones, rallied around their ancient banner by the very approach of peril, will make common cause with the slave Confederacy? In such a case, how avert the chances of a direful conflict? Will the United States carry patience with respect to the aggressors, the fear of giving a signal of ruin, deference to the counsels lavished on them perhaps, so far as to refuse to return a violent attack, and to consent to the ravishment of their capital? It is hard to believe. If the South make the attack, the war will break out, and the border States will be exposed to the first blow.

But admit that they succeed in preventing an immediate explosion, the mere fact of a total secession, and of the formation of two Confederacies, almost equal, (in appearance at least,) will permit no one to count on the prolonged preservation of peace. What repulsion, what grievances will be found in all relations, in all questions! And from a grievance to war, from war to negro insurrections, what will be the distance, I ask? The South will be then an immense powder magazine, to which the first spark will set fire. And the South will not lose its habits of arrogance, it will be quarrelsome as always. Has it not already announced in its journals that, on the first encouragement given to its fugitive slaves, it will draw the sword? Now, such encouragement certainly will not be wanting. The South does not know at the present time how much the North, of which it complains, contributes to prevent the escapes which it fears. The Federal Government is at hand to oppose them, in some measure at least. When the preventive obstacle shall have disappeared, the South will see with what rapidity its slavery will glide away on every point of its frontier; it will see its *happy* negroes ready to brave a thousand perils rather than remain under its law. Alas! it will see many other proofs of their devotion to servitude. I do not like to bring bloody images, at which I shudder, too often before the eyes of the reader; it must be said, notwithstanding, while it is yet time, that the general Confederacy of the South, intoxicated with its projects, resolved to increase its possessions, forced to demand from the African slave trade the means of repeopling its States, depopulated by escape, and to install slavery into new territories, will draw upon it, not only the wrath of the United States, but the indignation of the entire world. And what misery, what ruin will ensue from the first conflict!

I like better to fix my thoughts on the third

hypothesis—that of a return to the now broken Union. Taught by experience, recognizing how little weight it has in the world since its separation from the United States, poor, weak, divided, comprehending the impossibility of realizing its true plans without exposing itself to calamities, losing its resources, one after another, even to the cultivation of cotton, which also demands credit and security, incapable of preventing the flight of its slaves, and not daring to brave that great power of public opinion which will interdict it the African trade, the Southern Confederacy, exhausted and dismayed, will perhaps one day prefer returning to the bosom of the Union, to plunging into the extremity of misfortune. In this case, again, the question of affranchisement will have made vast strides. The United States will have taken a decided position in the absence of the South, which its return cannot destroy; convictions will be fixed, the final impulse will have been given, and to this impulse, the South, come to repentance, will know that nothing is left it but to submit.

Finally comes a last hypothesis, which I mention because it is necessary to foresee every possibility. Under the combined influence of the border States and the States of the North, equally desirous of maintaining the Union, the attempts of the extreme South will have failed, its secession will have lasted only a few months, and a compromise will have served to cover its retreat. But what compromise could compensate for a fact so important as the election of Mr. Lincoln? It has a deep significance which no compromise will remove; it signifies that the conquests of slavery are ended. This proven, the future is easy to foresee: increasing majorities in the North, increasing disproportion of the two parts of the Confederation. At the end of the four years of a Lincoln administration, the slave States will have lost all hope of struggling, with their eight thousand whites charged with keeping four millions of blacks, against the twenty millions of citizens that inhabit the free States. Let us add that, the future once fixed and the question of preponderance once resolved, many passions will moderate by degrees. The number of free States will increase, not only by the settling of new territories, but also by the affranchisement of the thinly scattered slaves, becoming continually more thinly scattered, of Maryland, of Delaware, or of Missouri. We can even now describe this affranchisement, so well is the *American method* known. It consists, as every one knows, in emancipating the children that are to be born.

This is the method which has been uniformly applied in the Northern States, and which will be doubtless applied some day in the border States, provided, however, civil war does not come to accomplish a very different emancipation—emancipation by the rising of the slaves. There will be nothing of this, I hope; pacific progress will have its way. We shall then see these intermediate States, one after the other, regaining life in the same time as liberty: they will become transformed as if touched by the wand of a fairy.

Such are the future prospects which offer themselves to us. If we remember, besides, the movement which is beginning to be wrought in the religious societies and the churches—a movement which cannot fail to be soon complete, we shall know on what to rely concerning the fate which awaits a social iniquity against which are at once conspiring the follies of its friends, and the indignation of its foes.

CHAPTER IX.

COEXISTENCE OF THE TWO RACES AFTER EMANCIPATION.

Something more difficult to foresee than the suppression, henceforth certain, of slavery, is the consequence of this suppression. The problem of the coexistence of the two races rests at the present hour with a crushing weight on the thoughts of all; it mingles poignant doubts with the hopes of some, it exasperates the resistance of others. Is it true that emancipation would be the signal of a struggle for extermination? Is there not room upon American soil for free blacks by the side of free whites? I do not conceal from myself that there is here an accredited prejudice, an admitted opinion which, perhaps more than any thing else, trammels the progress of the United States. Let us attempt to estimate it.

M. de Tocqueville, who has judged America with so sure an eye, has been, notwithstanding, mistaken upon some points; his warmest admirers must admit it. Writing at an epoch when the great results of English emancipation had not yet been produced, he was led to frame that formidable judgment of which so much advantage has been taken: "Hitherto, wherever the whites have been the more powerful, they have held the negroes in degradation and slavery; wherever the negroes have been the more powerful, they have destroyed the whites. This is the only account which can ever be opened between the two races."

Another account is opened, thank God, and no one will rejoice at it more sincerely than M. de Tocqueville—he who is so generous, and whose abolition sentiments are certainly no mystery to any of his colleagues of the Chamber. But his opinion remains in his book, and every one repeats after him, that the blacks and the whites cannot live together on the same soil, unless the latter be subject to the former.

I repeat, that at the time at which he wrote, he had reason, or at least known facts gave him reason, to say this; the liberty of the blacks had then but one name—St. Domingo. To-day, the victories of Christian emancipation have come, to contrast with the catastrophes provoked by impenitent despotism.

The English Colonies bear a striking analogy to the Southern States of the Union. The blacks there are numerous, more numerous even in proportion to the whites than in the Carolinas or Florida. The climate is even more scorching, and the cultures demand still more imperiously the labor of the blacks. As to the prejudices of the masters, I dare affirm that the planters of the Continent and those of the Antilles have not long had any thing with which to reproach each other. Notwithstanding, what has happened in the Antilles? Not only has liberty been proclaimed—this was the act of the metropolis—but the coexistence of races has subsisted. It is to this point that I claim attention. They, the whites and the blacks, alike free, invested with the same privileges, exercising the same rights, encountering each other in the ranks of the militia, in the magistracy, and even in the seats of the colonial assemblies, admirably accept this life in common. And the whites there, observe, are Anglo-Saxons; that is, they belong to that race which is declared incapable of enduring free blacks in its neighborhood.

It is necessary to appeal sometimes from those axioms so boldly laid down, which serve us to make inflexible laws for that which must be subject in an infinite measure to the mobility of circumstances and influences. The influence of the Gospel, especially, is a fact, the scope of which is never sufficiently measured. It has created in the Antilles a negro population which maintains its equality face to face with the whites, yet which does not entirely reject their patronage; a dependent population which is also a free population, free in the most absolute sense of the word. The blacks of the Antilles labor on the plantations, and secure the success of large plantations; but, at the same time, they themselves become landholders, forming by degrees one of the happiest and most remarkable classes of peasants that ever existed. Their little fields, their pretty villages, manifest real prosperity; and there is something among them that is worth more than prosperity, there is moral progress, the development of intellect, and the elevation of souls.

It will be demanded of us if, in the midst of so much progress, the production of sugar has not suffered. I answer that, on the contrary, it has increased. It had been predicted that emancipation would be a death-blow to the British colonies. I suspect that many people are even yet persuaded of it; now, in spite of the faults committed by the planters, who have neglected nothing to disgust the negroes with labor and to drive them from their old mills, they are found to return to them, contenting themselves with wages that scarcely rise above an average of a shilling a day. If we compare the two last censuses of liberty with the two last years of slavery, we shall discover that the total production of sugar has increased in the colonies in which emancipation was effected in 1834. And they have not only had to endure this crisis of emancipation, but also another crisis still more formidable, that of the sudden introduction of free trade in 1834. The colonial sugars, exposed to competition with the sugar produced at Havana and elsewhere by slave labor, experienced a prodigious decline. There was cause to believe that the production was about to be destroyed; it has risen again, notwithstanding, and the English Antilles, with their free negroes and their unprotected sugar, forced to face entire liberty in all its forms, import to-day into the metropolis nearly a million more hogsheads than at the moment when the crisis of free trade broke forth.

Liberty works miracles. We always distrust her, and she replies to our suspicions by benefits. The English Antilles, which, during the last thirty years, have had to surmount, besides the two crises of emancipation and free trade, the earthquake of 1840 and six consecutive years of drought; the English Antilles, which have had to liquidate their old debts, and to repair the ruin accruing from the failure of the bank of Jamaica, are now in an attitude which proves that they have no fears for the future and scarcely regret the past.

Under slavery, the Antilles were hastening to their ruin; with liberty, they have become one of the richest channels of exportation which England possesses; under slavery, they could not have supported the shock of free trade; with liberty, they have gained this new battle: such are the net proceeds of experience. If we still have doubts, let us compare Dutch Guiana, which holds slaves, to English Guiana, which has emancipated them. The resources of these two countries are almost equal; English Guiana is progressing, while the cultures of Surinam are forsaken; three-fourths of its plantations are already abandoned, and the rest will follow.

But the question of profits and losses is not the only one here, I think, and after having computed the proceeds of sugar, after having shown that in this respect English emancipation is in rule, it is allowable to mention also another kind of result.

Look at these pretty cottages, this neat and almost elegant furniture, these gardens, this general air of comfort and civilization; question these blacks, whose physical appearance has become modified already under the influence of liberty, these blacks, who decreased rapidly in numbers during the epoch of slavery, and who have begun to increase, on the contrary, since their affranchisement; they will tell us that they are happy. Some have become landowners, and labor on their own account, (this is not a crime, I imagine;) others unite to strengthen large plantations, or perhaps to carry to the works of rich planters the canes gathered by them on their own grounds; some are merchants, many hire themselves out as farmers. Whatever may be the faults of some individuals, the ensemble of free negroes has merited the testimony rendered in 1857 by the Governor of Tobago: "I deny that our blacks of the country are of indolent habits. So industrious a class of inhabitants does not exist in the world."

An admirable spectacle, and one which the history of mankind presents to us too rarely, is that of a degraded population elevating itself more and more, and placing itself on a level with those who before despised it. Concubinage, so general in times of servitude as to give rise to the famous axiom, "Negroes abhor marriage," is now replaced by regular unions. In becoming free, the negroes have learned to respect themselves: the unanimous reports of the governors mark the progress of their habits of sobriety. Crimes have greatly diminished among them. They are polite and well brought up, falling even into the excess of exaggerated courtesy. They respect the aged: if an old man passes through the streets, the children rise and cease their play.

These children are assiduously sent to schools, the support of which depends, in a great part, upon the voluntary gifts of the negroes. Grateful to the Gospel which has set them free, the former slaves have become passionately attached to their pastors; their first resources are consecrated to churches, to schools, and sometimes, also, to distant missions, to the evangelization of that Africa which they remember to do it good. We should be at once surprised and humiliated, were we to compare the much-vaunted gifts of our charity with those of these poor people, these freed men of yesterday, whom we think that we may rightfully treat with disdain.

Thanks to the Gospel, and it is to this that I

return, the problem of the coexistence of races is resolved in the most pacific manner in the Antilles. Among freemen, however little these freemen may be Christianized, specific inequalities become speedily effaced, and the prejudice of skin is not found to be ultimately as insurmountable as we have been told. In these English colonies, which are true republics, governing themselves, and which also remind us, through this feature, of the Southern States, the blacks have come to be accepted as fellow-citizens. They practise the liberal professions; they are electors and often elected, for they form of themselves alone one-fifth of the Colonial Assembly at Jamaica; they are officers of the police and the militia, and their authority never fails to be recognized by all. I named Jamaica just now. Some may seek to bring it as an argument against me. The fact is, that this great island has seemed to form an exception to the general prosperity; considerable fortunes have been sunk there, and the transformation has been slower and more painful there than elsewhere. But, when they arm themselves with these circumstances, they forget two things: first, that the causes of the malady were anterior to emancipation; next, that the cure has come from emancipation itself. Before emancipation, Jamaica was insolvent, her plantations were mortgaged beyond their value, and its planting was threatened in other ways far more than now. Do you know what has since happened? Difficulties which appeared insoluble have been resolved; to-day, the cape is doubled, and men navigate in peace. At the present time, Jamaica comprises two or three hundred villages, inhabited by free negroes; the latter are willing to work; for, according to the latest information, (February, 1861,) the price of daily labor decreases instead of rising. Among these free negroes, there are not less than ten thousand landholders, and three-eighths of the cultivated soil is in their hands. They have established sugar-mills everywhere, imperfect, rude, yet working in a passable manner; and mills of this sort are numbered by thousands. The middle class of color thus grows richer day by day; the families that compose it all own a horse or a mule; they have their bank books and their accounts with the savings banks. Lastly, which is of more value than all else, the free negroes of Jamaica have built more than two hundred chapels, and as many schools. At the very moment when I write these lines, an enthusiastic religious movement is prevailing among them; the rum-shops are abandoned, the most degraded classes enter in their turn the path of reformation.

I should have been glad to cite our own colonies instead of confining myself to the English islands. I have been prevented from this, not only by the memory of the conflagrations of 1859 at Martinique, and of the state of siege which it became necessary to proclaim there, but, above all, by the circumstance that the liberty of our former slaves has been too often restrained by means of the vagabond regulations, that labor has continued to be imposed on them to a certain point; that the parcelling out of property has been trammelled by fiscal measures; that, moreover, it is less the labor of our former slaves than of the Coolies and others employed, which has secured the success of our experiment; whence it follows that this success is far from being as conclusive as that which has been obtained elsewhere under the system of full liberty. Nevertheless, our success, which is no less real, signifies something also. If we have not yet those little free villages, that class of small negro landholders of which I just spoke, we have, like the English, free negroes in our militia and in our marine; like them, we have had our elections, and all classes of the population have taken part in them; like them, and perhaps in a greater degree, we have increased our sugar production since emancipation. It is true that the crisis of free trade has not yet passed among us, and that we cannot know how this would be supported by our colonial sugars. But it will not be long before we shall be informed on this point: by an act which we cannot but applaud, and which continues the work it has undertaken, the French government has just suppressed the protection continued hitherto to our planters. If, ere long, as it is justifiable to hope, they are delivered from the charges of the colonial system, whose advantages they have lost, we shall see them struggle, and successfully, I am convinced, against the Spanish sugars produced by slave labor.

It will be, perhaps, maintained, that the antipathy of race is stronger in the United States than elsewhere, and that the Americans, in this respect, are inferior to the English. I am as conscious as any one else of those infamous proceedings towards free negroes which are the crime of the North, a crime no less odious than that of the South. What conscience is not aroused at the thought of those prejudices of skin which do not permit blacks to sit by the side of whites, in schools, churches, or public vehicles? Only the other day, nothing less than a denunciation in open parliament was needed to begin the destruction, by a public rebuke, of the classification which is being made on the English steamers themselves between Liverpool and New York. There are some new States which purely and simply exclude free negroes from their Territory; those which do not exclude them from the Territory, repulse them from the ballot-box. The injustice, in fine, is as gross, as crying, as it is possible to imagine.

Must we conclude from this that the co-existence of races, possible elsewhere, is impossible in the United States? I distrust those sweeping assertions which resolve problems at one stroke; I refuse, above all, to admit so easily that iniquity must be maintained for the sole reason that it exists, and that it suffices to say: "I am thus made; what would you have? I cannot change myself," to abstract one's self from the accomplishment of the most elementary duty. To endure negroes at one's side, to respect their independence, to abstain from wrongs towards them, to consent to the full exercise of their rights, is an elementary duty; Christian duty, I need not say, demands something better.

Does this mean that we are to set ourselves up as judges, and brand as wretches all those who thus mistake the laws of charity and justice? I fear much that, in their place, we would do precisely as they. Living in the South, we would have slaves, and would defend slavery to the last; living in the North, we would tread under foot the free colored class. Is there then neither the true, nor the false, nor justice, nor injustice? God forbid! The just and the true remain; iniquity should be condemned without pity; but we are bound to be more indulgent towards men than towards things. We are bound to remember that the influence of surroundings is enormous, and that, if crimes are always without excuse, there are many excusable criminals.

When we examine men by the prejudice of skin, such as prevails in the United States, we are not long in discovering that it rests in great part on a misunderstanding: men mistake coexistence for amalgamation. I do not fear to affirm that the second would be as undesirable as the first would be desirable. Why dream of blending or of assimilating the two races? Why pursue as an ideal frequent marriages between them, and the formation of a third race: that of mulattoes? America does right to resist such ideas, and to inscribe her testimony against such a future, evidently very little in conformity with the designs of God.

But coexistence by no means draws amalgamation in its train. On this point, also, experience has spoken. In the English colonies, the liberty of the blacks is entire, the legal equality of the two races is not contested, public manners have shaped themselves to that mutual consideration without which they could not live together; yet neither amalgamation nor assimilation is in question, and the aristocracy of skin remains what it should be, a lasting distinction, accepted on both sides, between races which are not designed to mingle together. I do not know that many marriages are contracted between the whites and the negresses of Jamaica, and I believe that the class of mulattoes increases much more rapidly under slavery than with liberty. Look in this respect at what takes place even now in the United States: as quadroons sell better than blacks, mixtures of white or almost white slaves abound there, and the unhappy women who refuse to lend themselves to certain combinations are often whipped in punishment.

With liberty, each race can at least remain by itself; with it, there can be co-existence without amalgamation; both mingling and hostility can be prevented. This is the more easy, inasmuch as the negroes, with the gentleness of their race, willingly accept the second place, and by no means demand what we insist on refusing them. Let their liberty be complete, let legal equality and friendly relations be maintained, and they will ask no more.

But they will ask no less, and they are right. I do not understand, in truth, why so harmless a coexistence should be so long repulsed by the enlightened people of the United States. There are negroes in Spanish America who have reached the highest grades of the army, and who show as much intelligence, decorum, and dignity in command as white men could do. I myself have seen at Paris, a clergyman of ebony blackness, who was really the most distinguished, unexceptionable man that it was possible to meet; he was a remarkable scholar, and had received the title of doctor from several European universities.

In fact, the negroes are our fellows and our equals much more than we imagine; they adapt themselves better than the Indians to our civilization. They seek to be instructed, and not only do the free blacks of the English islands hasten, as we have seen, to provide themselves with teachers, but even those of the United States, crushed as they are by contemptuous treatment, neglect no means of introducing their children into the schools, where is found one-ninth of their total number. In Liberia, they have shown themselves hitherto very capable of ruling. In Hayti, since their deliverance from the ridiculous and odious yoke of Soulouque, they have advanced rapidly, it is affirmed, in the way of true progress; legal marriages increase, popular instruction is becoming established, religious liberty is respected. Lastly, in the negro colony of Buxton, in Canada, the fugitive slaves have become industrious landholders, and are respected by all.

Let us not say that prejudice of skin is indestructible; the suppression of slavery may modify it profoundly. What degrades the free negro to-day, is the existence of the negro slave. To be respectable, we all need to be respected. The poor, free negro is ashamed of himself; he dares not aspire to any thing noble and great; he preserves, besides, as the legacy of slavery, the idea that labor is dishonoring, that idleness is a sign of independence. This is enough to make him remain a stranger to honorable occupations, and confine himself to the practice of vile trades. When slavery shall have disappeared, the situation of the free blacks will become quite different: they will be numerous; they will have an appreciable share in the regulation of national affairs; their vote will count, and, thenceforth, we may be tranquil, no one will be afraid to treat them with respect, and perhaps to pay court to them.

The law of New York, as well as the Supreme Court of that State, has already admitted that color exercises no influence over the rights of citizens. The time draws near when the North will no longer contest the intervention of free negroes at the ballot-box. This will be a great step in advance. Let us remark, moreover, that, after general emancipation, the black population, while exercising its share of influence, will never be able, through the number of suffrages at its disposal, to alarm the jealous susceptibility of the whites; the latter, in fact, will be continually recruited by European immigration, and the day will come when the few negroes of the United States will be scarcely perceptible in the heart of a gigantic nation.

The honor of the North is at stake; it belongs to it to give an example at this time, and to show, by the reform of its own habits, that it has the right to combat the crime of the South. It must set to work seriously, resolutely, to resolve the problem of the coexistence of races, while the South resolves, willing or unwilling, the problem of emancipation. Liberty in the South, equality in the North; the one is no less necessary than the other; it may even be said that one great obstacle to the idea of emancipation is this other idea that blacks and whites cannot live together, but that one must some day exterminate the other.

Why suffer the establishment of this lying axiom which checks all progress? Why not cast our eyes on the neighboring colonies where the prejudice of color reigned supremely before emancipation, and where it has since become rapidly effaced. The United States have a lofty end to attain; let them beware how they take too low an aim! They will not have more than they need, with the efforts of all, the charity of all, the sacrifices of all, the earnest endeavors by which all can elevate themselves above vulgar prejudices, to accomplish a task at once the most difficult and most glorious that has ever been proposed to a great people.

The North, I repeat, is bound to give a noble example by obtaining a shining victory over itself. Let it say to itself that coexistence is not amalgamation; the question is not to marry negroes, but to treat them with justice. The fear of amalgamation once vanished, many things will change in appearance.

Why, in fact, is the prejudice of race stronger in the free States than in the slave States? Because the latter know that slavery is a sufficient line of demarcation, and because they have not to dread amalgamation. Now, this is and will be nowhere to be dreaded; the instinct of both races will prevent such mingling, and the blacks are as anxious to remain separate from the whites as the whites are to avoid alliance with the blacks. As I have said, nothing but slavery, and the perverse habits that it engenders, could have succeeded in some sort in breaking down this barrier. If the class of mullattoes thus formed rule in some republics of South America, it proceeds from the absence of a numerous and powerful white race, like that which is covering the United States with its continually increasing population.

Decidedly, fears of amalgamation are puerile in such a country; and decidedly also, any other solution than the coexistence of races would be wrong. Doubtless, a natural concentration of the emancipated negroes will be some day effected; they will flock to those States where their relative number will ensure to them the most influence. Perhaps we may even obtain a glimpse of the time when, by the result of a providential compensation, the countries which have been the witnesses of their sufferings, and which they have watered with their tears, these countries where they, better than any others, can devote themselves to labor, will belong to them in great part. Are the Antilles and the regions of the Gulf of Mexico destined to become the refuge and almost the empire of Africans torn from their own continent? It is possible, but not certain. In any case, this geographical repartition of the races would be wrought peaceably; the effort to effect it by violent measures would justly arouse the conscience of the human race. So long as we talk of transporting the blacks to Africa, to St. Domingo, or elsewhere, so long as the peaceable coexistence of the races be not accepted, the barbarous proceedings which dishonor America will not cease, the Northern States will maltreat their free negroes, and the South will cling to slavery as to the only means of preventing a struggle for extermination.

At the North as well as the South, men need to accustom themselves in fine to the idea of coexistence. Yes, there will be whites and free blacks in various parts of the Union; yes, it is certain that in some parts, the black population will be possessed of influence; it may even happen that, in one or two points of the extreme South, it will come to rule. If this hypothesis, improbable in my opinion, should ever be realized, it would not be a cause of shame, but of glory, to the Union. It is said that the great Indian tribes of the Southwest think of forming a State, which will demand admission into the Union, and which has a chance to obtain it. Why should there not be, at need, a negro State by the side of an Indian State? This reparation would be fully due to the oppressed race, and America would be honored in treading her repugnance under foot, and in showing to the whole world that her so much vaunted liberty is not a vain word.

She would show, at the same time, that her Christian faith is not a vain formality. If the desire of avoiding amalgamation has legitimate grounds, the antipathy of race is simply abominable. Words cannot be found severe enough to censure the conduct of those *Christians* who, pursuing with their indignation the slavery of the South, refuse to fulfil the simplest duties of kindness, or even of common equity, towards the free negroes of the North.

But I hope that the Gospel, accustomed to work miracles, will also work this. Let us be just; we have already seen the pious ladies of Philadelphia lavishing their cares on black and white without distinction at the time of the cholera invasion. They washed and dressed with their own hands, in the hospital which they had founded, the children rendered orphans by the scourge, without taking account of the differences of color. This is a sign of progress, and I could cite several others; I could name cities, Chicago, for instance, where the schools are opened by law to the blacks as well as the whites. There is a power in the United States which will overthrow the obstacle of the North as well as that of the South, which will abolish both slavery and prejudice of skin.

This power has shown in the Antilles what it can do. There, pastors and missionaries, schools, works of charity pursued in common, have placed on a level the blacks and the whites, devoted to the same cause, and ransomed by the same Saviour. In the United States, likewise, the Christian faith will raise up the one, and will teach the others to humble themselves; it will destroy the vices of the negro, and will break the detestable pride of the Anglo-Saxon. The real influence of faith on both—this is the true solution, this is the true bond of the races. Through this, will be established relations of mutual love and respect. What a mission is reserved for the churches of the United States!

Checked hitherto by enormous difficulties, which it would be unjust not to take into account, they have not acted the part in the recent struggle against slavery which reverted to them of right. They have done a great deal, whatever may be said; they are disposed to do still more, and their attitude has improved visibly within a year. But this cannot suffice; there are two problems to resolve instead of one; the question is now, to approach both face to face. True equality is founded, under the eye of God, through the community of hopes and of repentance, through close association in worship, in prayer, in action; and this equality has nothing in common with the jealous spirit of levelling which suffers old grievances to subsist, and continually invents new; it is peaceable, forgetful of evil, confiding, truly fraternal. I do not dream, of course, of the universal conversion of the population of the United States, both black and white; I know only that the Gospel, though it deeply penetrates comparatively few hearts, extends its influence much further, and acts on those that it has not won. Let the Christians of America set to work, let them reject, for it is time, the scandals still presented here and there by their apologists for slavery, let them forbear to spare that which is culpable, to call good evil, or evil good, and they will render to their country a service which they alone can render it, and to which nothing on earth can be compared.

The United States do not know how great will be the transformation of their internal condition, and the increase of their good renown abroad, when their churches, their schools, their public vehicles, their ballot-boxes, shall be widely accessible to persons of color, when equality and liberty shall have become realities on their soil; they do not know how great will be their peace and their prosperity. Let the two inseparable problems of slavery and the coexistence of races be resolved among them under the ruling influence of the Gospel, and they will witness the birth of a future far better than the past. No more fears, no more rivalries, no more separations in perspective, their conquests will become accomplished of themselves; and, no longer destined to swell the domain of servitude, they will win the applause of the entire world.

And all this will not be purchased, as men seem to believe, by the sacrifice of the cotton culture. At the present time, this culture incurs but one serious risk: the momentary triumph of a party that dreams of a slavery propaganda; it will be saved alone by the progress of liberty. On the day when emancipation shall be achieved, if wrought by the action of moral agents and social necessities, instead of by that of civil wars and insurrections, the cultivation of cotton in the Southern States will receive the impetus to a magnificent development. The emancipated negroes make large quantities of sugar in the Antilles; why should they not make cotton on firm ground? If affranchisement produced the destruction of planting in St. Domingo, we know now the reason. It is a proved fact that negroes who do not owe their liberty to insurrection, remain disposed to devote themselves to labor in the fields.

With slavery, observe, disappear, one after the other, the obstacles in the way of agricultural progress. The capital which no one dares risk to-day in the Southern States, will flow into them emulously as soon as slavery shall be abolished; I say more: as soon as its progressive abolition shall be no longer doubtful in the sight of all. European immigration, the current of which turns aside with so much circumspection, avoiding a territory accursed and given over to calamities, will flock towards those countries more beautiful, more fertile, and broader than those of the Far West. Machinery will come, to more than fill up the void caused by the passing diminution of the number of laborers. The slaves can be intrusted with none but the simplest implements: every one knows that the plough, introduced originally into our French colonies, disappeared to make room for the hoe as soon as Colbert had authorized the slave trade. Ploughs have reappeared there since emancipation. Their agricultural and industrial progress date from the same epoch: to-day, our colonists understand the use of manures, and make improvements in manufacture. A new era is dawning, in fine; what will it be in the United States, among that people which seems destined to surpass all others in the application of mechanics to agriculture?

Still, I have made one concession too much in admitting the diminution of the number of laborers. Supposing that a few negroes quit the field, many whites will come to take their place. White labor is fully possible in the majority of the slave States, and immigrants from Europe will not hesitate to engage in it. Wherever slavery reigns, it is that, and not the climate, that must be arraigned if the whites fold their hands; labor has become there a servile act—it is blighted, as it were, in its essence. A competent writer said the other day: "If Algeria had been subjected to the sway of slavery, cultivation there would have been reputed impracticable for the French, and examples of mortality would not have been wanting." The whites have labored in the Antilles; the whites can labor, not only in all the slave States of the intermediate region, but in Louisiana. Cotton is already produced in Texas, thanks to its German settlers. The question is only, to go on in this way. Slavery once abolished, the small proprietors, who at present carry all the criminal extravagancies of the South further than any others, will be compelled to set their hands to work. This will be an advantage both to the country and themselves. Who will not pray for the coming of the time when so considerable a part of the population will cease to possess slaves which it is incapable of feeding, when it will be transformed into the middle class, and thus escape the real servitude which embitters it?

Moreover, let us not forget new cultures, that of the vine among others, which are fitted to become introduced into these new countries, or to develop there, and which lack nothing but liberty in order to flourish. The arts and manufactures also have their place; independently of the tillers of the soil, properly called, the Southern States will have need of workmen in manufactories, and of managers of agricultural machines; large plantations will often become divided, as has happened in the Antilles, and we shall witness the appearance of the small estate, that essential basis of social order. There will be employment for all, and the rich Southern cultures will be less neglected than before.

Whoever has descended the Ohio has involuntarily compared its two banks: here, the State of Ohio, whose prosperity advances with rapid strides; there, the State of Kentucky, no less favored by Nature, yet which languishes as if abandoned. Why? Because slavery blights all that it touches. Could not the whites of Kentucky and Virginia labor as well as those of Ohio? The comparative poverty of these slave States reminds me of the destitution of our colonies and those of England before emancipation: mortgaged estates, plantations burdened with expenses, the complete destruction of credit—such was their position. We must read American statistics to form an idea of the truly unheard-of extent of this fact—impoverishment by slavery. With a larger extent and much richer lands, the slave States possess neither agricultural growth, nor industrial growth, nor advance of population, which can be compared far or near with that which is found in the free States. A book by Mr. Hinton Rowan Helper, *The Impending Crisis of the South*, expresses these differences in figures so significant that it is impossible to contest them.

The Southern States, therefore, are certain to increase their cultures, and to found their lasting prosperity by entering the path that leads to emancipation. But if they take the contrary road, they will hasten to their destruction, and with strange rapidity. Already, their violent acts of secession, and the monstrous plans which are necessarily attached to them, have had the first effect, easily foreseen, of dealing a most dangerous blow to American cotton. In a few weeks, they have done themselves more harm than the North, supposing its hostility as great as it is little, could have done them in twenty years. The meeting of Manchester has replied to the manifestoes of Charleston; England has said to herself, that, from men so determined to destroy themselves, she should count on nothing; and, having taken her resolution, she will proceed with it speedily; let the Southern States take care. English India can produce as much cotton as America; before long, if the Carolinians persist, they will have obtained the glorious result of despoiling their country of its chief resource; they will have killed the hen that laid the golden eggs. The matter is serious; I ask them to reflect on it. As England, under pain of falling into want and riots, cannot dispense with cotton for a single day, she will act energetically. Cotton grows marvellously in many countries; in the Antilles, where it has been produced already; in Algeria, where the plantations are about to be increased; on the whole continent of Africa, in fine, where it enters perhaps into the plans of God thus to make a breach in indigenous slavery by the faults committed by slaveholders in America.

CHAPTER X.

THE PRESENT CRISIS WILL REGENERATE THE INSTITUTIONS OF THE UNITED STATES.

It remains for me to inquire what influence the present crisis may exert on the institutions of the United States. It is at the expense of these institutions that the slave States, inferior in strength, in numbers, in progress of every kind, would reëstablish their fatal and growing preponderance. Here again, therefore, my thesis subsists: the victories of the South had compromised every thing, the resistance of the North is about to save every thing; the election of Mr. Lincoln is a painful but salutary crisis, it is the first effort of a great people rising.

The party of slavery had introduced into the heart of American democracy, a permanent cause of debasement and corruption. In this respect, also, it was leading the Confederation to its death by the most direct and speedy way. I wish to show

10*

how it developed the worst sides of the democratic system. I hope to be impartial towards this system; although persuaded that the government of which England offers us the model is better suited to guaranty public liberties and to second true progress in every thing, I am not of those who place the shadow before the substance, and who condemn democracy without appeal. Are we destined some day to pass into its hands? Have we already begun to glide down the descent that leads to it? It is possible. In any case, it would be unjust to hate America on account of it, as is too often done. America has had no choice; in virtue of its origin and its history, it could be nothing else than a democracy. If it has the faults of democracy, the unamiable rudeness, the violent proceedings, the levelling passions, I am scarcely surprised at it. I ask myself rather if it has known how to find a basis of support against the temptations of such a system, if it has prevented the subjugation of individuals by the mass, the absorption of consciences by the State, the substitution of the sovereignty of the end for that of the people. These are the shoals of democracy; have they been shunned by the United States? Have they been able to avoid transforming it either into tyranny or socialism? We shall see that, if it has not succumbed to the temptation, this has not been the fault of the party of slavery. Thanks to it, the corruption of democratic institutions was rapidly advancing; a single adversary, constantly the same, has combated the progress of this work of destruction. We shall encounter again, upon the ground of political institutions, the fundamental antagonism of the Gospel and slavery.

I say first, that it is rarely that names are altogether fortuitous, and do not correspond to things. It has often given rise to astonishment that the party of slavery should have taken the name of the democratic party; notwithstanding, nothing was more natural. How could slavery have been defended if not by exaggerating democracy? It was necessary, in such a cause, to deny the notions of right, of truth, and of justice; it was necessary that the greater number should become right, truth, and justice.

Something more even was needed. The *sovereignty of the end* must yield, if necessary, before the sovereignty of numbers. A cause like that of slavery is only defended in the heart of a democratic nation, by teaching it contempt of scruples, and the stifling of the conscience. Every thing is allowable, every thing is good, provided that we succeed in our ends! This is the rule which it designs shall prevail in political contests. A single question, seeing nothing but itself, determined to spare nothing, offering itself to parties, whoever they may be, who seek a change, creating factitious majorities to effect the ends of base ambition, taking account neither of honor nor country, and attaining its end through every thing—this is enough to vitiate profoundly institutions and morals. The sovereignty of the idea, when it has laid hands on the sovereignty of the people, is in a position to go to great lengths, and to sink very low. Moral maxims and written laws are trodden under foot, a struggle without pity or remorse begins, a struggle of life and death. Social passions easily acquire a degree of perversity which political passions do not possess; the former are without conscience and without compassion; they will be satisfied, cost what it may; triumph is in their eyes an absolute, an inexorable necessity. Rather than not conquer, they will rend the country.

What the regular working of institutions becomes under such a pressure, every one can divine. For some years past, in proportion as the pretensions of the slavery party had increased, we had seen public morals become tainted in the United States.

Indifference to means had made alarming progress, and had been felt even in the habits of commerce, and the relations of private life. The spirit of enterprise had come to be exalted even in its most dishonorable acts; respect for bankrupts seemed almost to be propagated. It is a fact, that men like Mr. Jefferson Davis, the present President of the revolted South, were not afraid to recommend the repudiation of debts. In the school of slavery, a disembarrassed and unscrupulous manner of acting had given its stamp to the general manner of the nation. Affairs were going on rapidly, the liberties of America were on the high road to ruin; it was time that the reaction of liberal and honorable sentiments should make itself felt. The election of 1860 marked the stopping-place.

I wonder that they could have stopped; such a fact demands an explanation, for ordinarily the declivities of democratic decline are never remounted. The natural tendency there being to deny the right of the minority, (the most precious of all,) to sink the man entire in the ballot, to lay violent hands on the private portion of his life, and to force even his conscience into the social contract, it follows that governments arise in which the question of limitation becomes effaced by the question of origin. In the face of such a power, nothing is left standing; no more rights, no more principles, no more of those solid and resisting blocks which serve to stem the popular current; the province of the State becomes indefinite.

And how much more irresistible and more perverse is this tendency, when a profound cause of corruption, such as slavery, adds its action to the strength of such democracies! It is no longer, in such cases, the sovereign majority alone before which the right may be forced to bow, it is a party determined to attain its ends, which penetrates with violence into that domain of conscience where human laws should not enter; a party which sets about regulating sometimes the belief, sometimes the thought, sometimes the speech. Such has been the influence exercised in the United States by the institution of slavery; it has forbidden authors to write, clergymen to preach, and almost individuals to think any thing that displeased it; it has invented the right of secession, in order to have at its disposal a formidable means of intimidation, and to place a threat behind each of its demands. To yield, to descend, to descend still further, to obey a continued impulse of democratic debasement, such is the course to which it has impelled the whole Confederation.

Notwithstanding, the United States have resisted. I shall tell why; I shall show by virtue of what marvellous force Americans have escaped the absolute levelling which seemed destined to be produced by a complicated democracy of slavery. But I wish first to finish depicting the natural effects of such a system.

Suppose for a moment a nation (and such are not wanting) modelled after the antique. The Pagan principle reigns there supremely, the State absorbs every thing, souls are banded together and governed; a centralized power, a visible Providence, is substituted for individual action; creeds have essentially the hereditary and national form; each one believes what the rest believe, each one does what the rest do, each one holds the opinions which are found in the ancient traditions of the country; truth is no longer a personal conviction, acquired at the price of earnest struggles, and worth much because it has cost much; it descends to the rank of customs to which it is fitting to conform, it has its marked place among social obligations, and forms part of the duties of the citizen.

Let democracy come to establish its empire in the heart of such a nation, and you will see with what rapidity every thing will disappear that bears the slightest resemblance to individual independence. The more effectual the levelling, the greater will seem the community; and the smaller the individual, the more, too, in face of the privileges of the whole, will the very idea of personal rights become effaced. The majority is held infallible, and the minority appears criminal if it takes the liberty of refusing to subject its thoughts (yes, its very thoughts) to that of the majority. In this innumerable host of like beings, no one is authorized to possess any thing in private; of all aristocracies, that of the conscience appears then least endurable. Men believe in the majority, in the mass, in the nation. We have no idea of the intellectual despotism of a democracy which fails to encounter on its road the obstacle of personal convictions; it disposes of the human soul, it creates an unlimited confidence in the judgment of public opinion, it heads a school of popular courtiers, and teaches each one the art of setting his watch by the clock of the market-place.

Intelligence, conscience, convictions—all bend, and what does not bend is broken. This happens, above all, we repeat without wearying, when a detestable cause like that of slavery perverts the working of democratic institutions. Then, the tyranny of the majorities has no bounds; the majorities themselves are formed by means of ignoble contracts and monstrous alliances. In the midst of lower passions let loose, through banded parties, imperative mandates, and factitious organizations, which no longer leave the smallest outlet for the flight of the least independent wish, the perversities of corrupt and misled democracy have full scope.

In writing these pages, have I described American democracy? Yes and no. Yes, for such are really the temptations to which America has been exposed, such are really the vices with which it might have often been reproached; no, for a principle of resistance has always revealed itself in the darkest moments, an irrepressible something has always remained. In vain the heavy roller has passed and repassed over the ground; it has always encountered blocks of granite that would not be broken. This is the point which I had at heart to signal out in closing this study, knowing that it forms its most essential part, and that whoever has not given it his attention cannot comprehend the United States. The extraordinary fact, much more extraordinary than is supposed, that, under the system of democracy ruled by slavery, men have been able to pause and retrace their steps, is only explained by the peculiar form which religious belief has put on in the United States. We have not before our eyes a Latin nation, a nation clad in the vestments of Greece or Rome, a nation having, according to the ancient mode, its religion and its usages universally but indolently admitted. This republic of the New World is by no means one of those slave republics of ancient times, in which the citizens took delight in conversing on public affairs, but in which no one had the bad taste to question his conscience with respect to the public creeds. The pagan life, with its obligatory worship, its common education, its suppression of the family and the individual in behalf of the State, its existence transported to the Forum; the pagan life, in which the citizen absorbs the individual, and in which the calm and serene uniformity of indifferent centuries ends, by giving to each one the national physiognomy, bears no resemblance to the moral and social life of the United States.

Among them, not the smallest trace is found of that system which seeks to make nations, and which forgets to make men. They were born, as we may say, of a protestation of the human conscience. A noble origin, which explains many things! It is, in fact, the revindication of religious independence against religious uniformity, and the established church which created it two hundred years ago. Of course, I have not to examine here the intrinsic value of the Puritan doctrines. I content myself with affirming that they landed in America in the name of liberty, that they were destined to establish liberty there, that they were destined to build there the true rampart against democratic tyranny.

From the first day, the State was deprived of the direction of the intellectual and moral man. Despite that inevitable mixture of inconsistencies and hesitation which marks our first efforts in all things, the Puritan colonies, destined one day to become the United States, set out on the road which led to liberty of belief, of thoughts, of speech, of the press, of assemblage, of instruction. The most considerable, most important rights were abstracted at the outset from the domain of democratic deliberations; insuperable bounds were set to the sovereignty of numbers; the right of minorities, that of the individual, the right of remaining alone against all others, the right of being of one's own opinion, was reserved. Furthermore, they did not delay to break the bonds between the Church and the State entirely, in such a manner as to deprive the official superintendence of belief of its last pretext. Self-government was founded, that is, the most formal negation of subjugation by the democracy. While the latter tends to the maximum of government, the American Government tends to the minimum of government, that form *par excellence* of liberalism. And it does not tend thither, as in the Middle Ages, by anarchy, by the absence of national ties, and moreover by despoiling the individual of his rights of conscience and thought, confiscated then more entirely for the benefit of a sovereign church than they have been since for the benefit of the State; no, American individualism proceeds differently: if it restrains with salutary vigor the province of governments, it is to enlarge that of the human soul.

This is a great conquest; the whole future of the modern world is contained in it. Destined as we are to submit, in a measure at least, to the action of democracy, the question whether we shall be slaves or free men is resolved in this: shall we, after the example of America, have our reserved tribunal, our closed domain in which the public power shall be permitted to see nothing? Shall there be things among us (the most important of all) which shall not be put to the vote? Shall our democracy have its boundaries, and beyond these boundaries shall a vast country be seen to extend—that of free belief, of free worship, of free thought, of the free home?

It is because American democracy has boundaries that its worst excesses have finally found chastisement. It is not installed alone in the United States; opposite it, another power which knows no fear, is occupied with resisting it. The entire history of America is explained by this double fact: the falling and the rising again, the servitudes and the liberties, the too long triumph of the slavery party, and the recent victory of Mr. Lincoln, the deadly peril so lately incurred, and the noble future that opens to-day.

Individualism is not isolation, individual convictions are not sectarian convictions; they found on the contrary the most powerful of the unities, moral unity. The thing which most actively dissolves societies while seeming to unite them, is the uniformity of national dogmas which, accepted as an inheritance, remain without action over the heart. What are, in fact, the great bonds on earth, if not duty and affection? Now, nothing but personal convictions, earnestly acquired by the sweat of our brow, can destroy selfishness in us. Without this strong cement of convictions at once individual and common, you will build nothing that will endure. The United States have in their heart strong convictions, which are also common convictions;

through external diversities, we have seen that fundamental conformity is real, and all earnest appeal to Christian truths agitates this country, so divided in appearance, from one end to the other. National life is here a reality. I do not think that Socialism, which excuses us from believing ourselves, which places our soul under responsible administration, and preserves us, it is said, from the baleful disruptions engendered by individualism, succeeds as well in destroying selfishness and in diffusing ideas of devotion and duty. When democracy becomes socialistic, (and it never has been able to become so in the United States,) it grinds down and reduces souls to such a degree that nothing is left but a fine dust, a sort of intellectual and moral powder which, it is true, is an obstacle to nothing, but which creates nothing either. To build an edifice, stones are needed, sand will not suffice.

Christian individualism makes the stones, and the democratic party has just perceived it. In a country where independence of soul has acclimated independence in all its forms, men may indeed bow the head sometimes to democracy allied to slavery; but this debasement has a limit, and the time is coming when they will raise their heads. Strong beliefs are a strong rampart, the slaves of truth are free men, and true independence begins in the heart. To have convictions in order to have characters, to have believers in order to have citizens, to have energetic minds in order to have powerful nations, to have resistance in order to have support —such is the programme of individualism. Show me a country where men are proud enough not to bow before the majority, where they do not think themselves lost when they depart from the beaten track, and jostle of received opinions; and I will admit that there it will be possible to practise democracy without falling into servitude.

There is but one country of individual belief, that could attempt the alliance, hitherto deemed impossible, of democracy and liberty. The theory in accordance with which the public liberties of England have the aristocracy for their essential basis, is admitted as an axiom; without contemning this element of social organization, it is advisable to mine deeper than this to discover the true foundation of liberty. Individual belief—this is the foundation. The more we reflect, the more we discover that the essential thing is not the forms of government, or even the relations of the different classes, but the moral state of the community. Are men there? Have souls become masters of themselves? Are characters formed? Has the force of resistance appeared? Whoever shall have replied to these questions will have decided, knowingly or unknowingly, whether liberty be possible.

I do not know that any people should be excluded from liberty; only all are bound to pursue it by the path that leads to it, by earnestness of convictions, by internal affranchisement, which signifies by the Gospel. We may seek in vain, we shall find no means comparable to this (I speak in the political point of view) when the question is to make citizens. To place one's self under the absolute authority of God and his word, is to acquire in the face of mere parties, majorities, general opinions, an independence that nothing can supply. The independence within is always translated without; he who is independent of men, in the domain of beliefs and of thoughts, will be equally so in the domain of public affairs. Thus democracy itself will not degenerate into socialism. No one has been able to point out the slightest symptom of socialism in the United States. Notwithstanding, democracy is fully complete there, and the election of Mr. Lincoln, once drover, once flatboatman, once rail-splitter, once clerk—of Mr. Lincoln, the son of his works, who has succeeded by his own powers in becoming a well-informed man and an orator, this election proves certainly that American equality is not menaced by the success of the republican party. It menaces only the evil democracy, which, under the guidance of the slavery party, sought to force the nation into the path of socialism. But it will not succeed in this; the question has just been decided. Between these two systems, which are to contend for contemporaneous communities, between socialism and individualism, the choice of the United States is made.

Before witnessing the affranchisement of the slaves, we shall, therefore, witness the affranchisement of American politics. They have endured a shameful yoke, and received sad lessons. Since Jefferson, the born enemy of true liberalism, founded the Democratic party, the United States had continued to descend the declivity of radicalism; a work of relentless levelling was thenceforth pursued, and the domain of the conscience became gradually invaded. The democratic party found its fulcrum in the South. The slave States forced the enclosure of the private tribunal, and confiscated in behalf of the State the inviolable rights of the individual: neither thought, the press, nor the pulpit, were free among them; the fundamental maxims of Puritan tradition were sacrificed by them one after the other. They did more: thanks to them, men were beginning to learn in the free States how to set to work to pervert their own consciences, and to substitute for it respect for sovereign majorities. Every day, crying iniquities were covered by the pretext: "If we were just, we should compromise the national unity, or we should risk losing the votes secured to our party." Violence, menace, brutality, and corruption, were boldly introduced into political struggles. Men became habituated to evil: the most odious crimes, the Southern laws reducing to legal slavery every free negro who should not quit the soil of the States, hardly raised a murmur of disapprobation; the United States seemed on the point of losing that faculty which nothing can survive—the faculty of indignation.

Behold in what school the democratic party had placed the American people—that noble people which, despite the grave faults with which it may be reproached, represents in the main many of the lofty principles which are allied to the future of modern communities. The reign of the Democratic party would form the subject of an inglorious history; in it we should see figure the glorification of servitude, piracy applied to international right, and, in conclusion, those facts of corruption and waste which served to crown its last Presidency. The most consistent champions of the doctrines and practices of the democratic party, are those men who have just declared that votes are valid only on condition of giving the majority to slavery, and that a regular election is a sufficient cause for separation.

CONCLUSION.

I HAVE not sought to recount events, but to attempt a study, which I believe to be useful to us, and which may, also, not be useless to the United States. We owe them the support of our sympathy. It is more important than people imagine to let them hear words of encouragement from us at this decisive moment. Let us not hasten to declare that the Union is destroyed, that, henceforth and forever, there will be two Confederacies existing on the same footing, that the United States of slavery will have their great *rôle* to perform here below, like the United States of liberty. This would be, in any case, immense exaggeration. Let us not forget that the Union has often before seemed lost, that the Confederation has often before seemed ready to perish. Are the men who are terrified at the present perils, ignorant of those which surrounded the cradle of the United States: mutinous troops, contending ambitions, threats of separation, anarchy, ruin? This America, then so weak, is the same that has since become so strong, in spite of its own faults. At the moment when it rebelled against England, it had neither arts and manufactures, nor commerce, nor marine; and its two or three millions of inhabitants were far from agreeing among themselves. Yet such is the vigor of its genius, such is its carelessness of every kind of danger, such is the impetuosity with which it affronts and surmounts obstacles, such is the power of its national motto, "Go ahead!" that through internal struggles, crises, and momentary exhaustion, it has attained the stature of a great people. Count the steamboats on its rivers, estimate the tonnage of its vessels, compute the amount of its internal trade, measure the length of its canals and railroads, and you will still have but a faint idea of what it is capable of undertaking and accomplishing.

We must remember these things, and not imitate those enemies of America who sometimes feign to put on mourning for her, sometimes jest at her distress, and find in the present situation of the *disunited States* (for thus they style them) an agreeable subject for pleasantry, forgetting that this disunion has a serious cause, which is certainly of importance enough to make itself understood; forgetting, too, that generous struggles for humanity and the country are worthy to obtain our fullest respect. And let us beware how we say that this crisis does not concern us—that we can do nothing in it. The selfish isolation of nations is henceforth impossible. The question to be decided here involves our own affairs, not only because a portion of our fortune is pledged to the United States, but, above all, because our principles and our liberties are concerned. The victories of justice, wherever they may be won, are the victories of the human race.

We can aid this one in some measure. America, which affects sometimes to declare itself indifferent to our opinions, gathers them up, however, with jealous care. I have seen respectable Americans blush at encountering that instinctive blame which, among us, is addressed to the progress of slavery; they suffered at seeing their country thus fallen from the esteem which it formerly enjoyed. Proud nations like America always avenge themselves by noble impulses for the reprobation which they are conscious of having deserved. The moral intervention of Europe is not, therefore, superfluous; it is the less so, in that the South insults us by counting on us. The ringleaders of Charleston and New Orleans affect to say that England is ready to open her arms to them, and that France promises a sympathizing reception to her envoys! These envoys themselves have been selected with care, honorable, having friends among us,—capable, in a word, of presenting the cause of slavery in an almost seductive light. It is important, therefore, that we should not keep silence.

Let governments be reserved; let them avoid every thing that would resemble direct action in the internal affairs of the United States, let them have recourse to the commonplaces of speech employed by diplomacy to escape pledging their policy—this is well. But to imagine that these commonplaces promise alliance or protection, is to be credulous indeed! A rebellion under cover of the flag of slavery, be sure, will find it difficult to make partisans among us French, whatever may be our indolent indifference in other respects in this matter, an indifference so great that at the present time the American question *does not exist* to the most of us. Moreover, we shall shake off this inertia; and, as to the English, they will not suffer their brightest title to glory in modern times to be tarnished by any latent complicity with the Gulf States. The brutal doctrines of interest, so often professed publicly in Parliament by Mr. Bright, may indeed find organs;

and Great Britain will be counselled to remember cotton and forget justice. The measure already taken by her at Washington, and which appears to have been supported by France, a measure designed to declare that the blockade of the Southern ports must be effectual to be recognized, is perhaps a concession wrested from her by this detestable school of selfishness. Happily, there is another school face to face with this; the Christian sentiment, the sentiment of abolition, will arise and enforce obedience. Never was a more important work in store for it. To unveil every suspicious act of the British Government, to keep public opinion aroused, to maintain, in fine, that noble moral agitation which makes the success of good causes and the safety of free nations, such is the mission proffered in England to the defenders of humanity and the Gospel. If they could forget it, the populace of Mobile or Savannah pursuing English consuls, would remind them to what principle the name of Great Britain is inevitably pledged, for the sake of its honor. France and England, I am confident, will act in unison, here as elsewhere; their alliance which comprises within itself the germs of all true progress, will be found as useful and as fruitful in the New World as it has proved in the Old.

This is of such importance that I beg leave to dwell on it; evidently our influence has not yet been exercised as it should have been, and if Mr. Lincoln now bends somewhat before counsels devoid of energy and dignity, it proceeds in part from our reserve, our silence, our apparent neutrality—who knows? even from the discouraging language that has been sometimes held in our name. The publication of the unlucky Morrill Tariff, (signed, we may say in passing, by Mr. Buchanan, and the revocation of which, I am convinced, will be signed some day by Mr. Lincoln,) has given the signal for political demonstrations, all of which are very far from being to the credit of Europe. Our *Moniteur* has published articles to be regretted, but it is above all among the English that the cotton party has had full scope.

Let England beware! it were better for her to lose Malta, Corfu, and Gibraltar, than the glorious position which her struggle against slavery and the slave trade has secured her in the esteem of nations. Even in our age of armed frigates and rifled cannon, the chief of all powers, thank God! is moral power. Woe to the nation that disregards it, and consents to immolate its principles to its interests! From the beginning of the present conflict, the enemies of

England, and they are numerous, have predicted that the cause of cotton will weigh heavier in her scales than the cause of justice and liberty. They are preparing to judge her by her conduct in the American crisis. Once more, let her beware!

And under what pretexts do we chaffer with the government of Mr. Lincoln for those energetic, persevering sympathies on which it has a right to count? Let us examine.

We hear, in the first place, of the vigor of the South and the weakness of the North. It is not the first time that a bad cause has shown itself more ardent, more daring, less preoccupied by consequences, than a good one. Good causes have scruples, and every scruple is an obstacle.

I am assuredly as sorry as any one to see Mr. Lincoln struck with a sort of paralysis. To my mind, the dangers of inactivity are considerable; I believe that it discourages friends and encourages adversaries; I believe that it sanctions more or less the baleful and erroneous principle of secession, a principle more contagious than any other; I believe, in fine, that, by postponing civil war, it probably risks increasing its gravity. Nevertheless, shall we not take into account the exceptional difficulties with which Mr. Lincoln is surrounded?

The preceding Administration took care to leave no resource in his hands: he found the forts either surrendered or indefensible, the arsenals invaded, the army scattered, the navy despatched to distant parts of the seas. Is it strange that he should have yielded in some degree to the entreaties of so many able men, all urging in the same direction? If to-morrow he should yield entirely, if he should recognize the Southern Confederacy, would it be great cause for astonishment?

Let us not forget, moreover, that the border States are at hand, forming a rampart, as it were, to protect the extreme South. Several of these States, I am convinced, incline sincerely towards the North, and will remain united with it; but are there not others, Virginia, for instance, which perhaps only refrain from seceding for the better protection of those that have done so, and whose present rôle consists in preventing all repression, while its future rôle will be to trammel all progress by the continued threat of joining the Southern Confederacy?

These are serious obstacles; yet I have not pointed out the most serious of all—the intense and sincere repugnance which many Northern people, though declared adversaries of slavery, experience towards measures that are calculated to provoke slave insurrections, and endanger the safety of the planters. I must acknowledge that the patience of the strong seems here rather more laudable than the so much vaunted audacity of the weak, who count on this patience, and know that they can be arrogant without much risk.

The second pretext that is audaciously brought forward to solicit our good will towards the South, is that it has just ameliorated the Federal institutions. Let us ask in what consists this pretended amelioration? The South has not feared to write in set terms, in its fundamental law, what none before it ever dared write, *the constitutional guarantee of slavery*. Slavery, in accordance with the Constitution of the South, can neither be suppressed nor assailed. Slavery will be the holy ark to be regarded with respect from afar off, the corner-stone which all are forbidden to touch. By the side of this, the South ostentatiously proclaims freedom of speech, of the press, of discussion in every form! Men shall be free to speak, but on condition of not touching, nearly or remotely, on any subject connected with slavery, (and every thing is connected with it in the South.) They shall be free to print, but on condition of giving no writing whatever to the public from which may be inferred the unity of mankind, the sanctity of family ties, the great principles, in fact, which the "patriarchal system" throws overboard. They shall be free to discuss, but on condition of not disturbing this institution, impatient by nature, and still more so in future, now that it feels itself hemmed in and threatened on all sides. It will be by itself alone the whole Constitution of the South; this one article will devour the rest; in default of legislatures and courts, the Southern populace know how to give force to the guarantee of slavery, and to restrain freedom of speech, of the press, and of discussion.

It is true that adroit patrons of the South Carolinian rebellion have a third argument at their service which is no less specious. "All is over," they exclaim, "there is nobody now to sustain, there are no sympathies now to testify; in four days, peace will be made, the new Confederation will be recognized by Lincoln in person, a commercial treaty will even ally it to the United States: the affair is ended."

The affair is scarcely begun, we answer; one must be blind not to see it. What is ended, is only the first skirmish. As to the war, it will be as long, believe me, as the life of the two principles which are struggling in America. Let Mr. Lincoln assure himself, and let the European adversaries of slavery remember as well, that it will be necessary to combat and to persevere. Never was a more obstinate and more colossal strife commenced on earth. Many of the border States will not be long in raising pretensions to which they will join threats of new secessions; they will again bring up the question of the Territories, and will propose compromises. Who knows? they will aspire perhaps to establish, in the interests of the extreme South, the extradition of slaves escaped from the rival Confederacy. Who knows again? they will perhaps attempt to restore their domestic slave trade with Charleston and New Orleans.

This is not all. The time will come when the extreme South, incapable of enduring the life that it has just created for itself, will demand to return to the bosom of the Union. It will then insist on dictating its conditions; it will propose the election of a general convention charged with reconstructing the Constitution of the United States; it will appeal to the selfishness of some, and to the ambition or even the patriotism of others, presenting to their sight the re-establishment of the common greatness which separation had compromised.

What a motive to veil principles for a moment! what a temptation to return to the fatal path so lately forsaken!

I know very well that it will be henceforth impossible to return to it completely; nevertheless, the vigilance of Mr. Lincoln will not cease to be necessary, and what will be no less necessary, is the moral support which we are bound to lend him in the hour of success and in the hour of discouragement, in good and in bad reputation. Where do we find a more glorious cause than this? despite the impure alloy which is mingled with it, of course, as with all glorious causes, is it not fitted to stir up generous hearts? Already, thanks to the defeat of the democratic party, the United States that we once knew, those of the last ten years, those that the South governed with its wand, those whose institutions were corrupted and debased by slavery, those who numbered in the North as in the South so many fortunes based openly on the slave traffic, those who had seen among their Presidents a slave merchant, carrying on his speculations in public view—these United States have just ended their career, they have entered the domain of history, their disappearance has been verified by the retreat of the extreme South.

The American people are now striving to rise. Enterprise as difficult as glorious! Whatever may be the issue of the first conflict, it will be only the first conflict. There will be many others; the uprising of a great people is not the work of a day. Sometimes at peace, sometimes perhaps at war with the States that take in hand the cause of slavery, the American Confederation will witness the development, one after another, of the consequences necessarily produced by that decisive event, the election of Mr. Lincoln. Having broken with the past, it will be forced to enter further and further into the path of the future. We have already seen that, whichever hypothesis is realized of those which we are permitted to foresee, the cause of slavery is destined to experience defeat after defeat. It has ceased to grow, it is about to decrease, to decrease by separation, to decrease by union, to decrease by peace, to decrease by war. As surely as there will be obstacles without number to surmount in order to accomplish this work, so surely will this work be accomplished. Certainly, it deserves to be loved and sustained, without discouragement and hesitation. Europe will comprehend it.

On seeing her attitude, the angry champions of

slavery will doubtless perceive that they are mistaken, and that it is time to make new calculations. As for the brave men of the North, they will be glad to learn what is thought of them on this side of the Atlantic. This may aid, and greatly, in the more or less distant re-establishment of the Union. If the Gulf States knew what insurmountable disgust will be aroused here by their Confederacy, founded to secure the duration and prosperity of slavery; if the border States knew what sympathies they will gain by siding with liberty, and what maledictions they will incur by declaring themselves for slavery; if the Northern States knew what support is secured to them by that power, the chief of all others, public opinion, we are justified in believing that the present crisis would come to a prompt and peaceful solution.

It is a fixed fact that the nineteenth century will see the end of slavery in all its forms; and woe to him who opposes the march of such a progress! Who is not deeply impressed by the thought that, on the 4th of March, at the very hour when Mr. Lincoln, in taking possession of the Presidency at Washington, signified to the attentive world the will of a great republic, determined to arrest the conquests of slavery, the generous head of a great empire signified to his ministers his immutable resolve to prepare for the emancipation of the serfs. In such coincidences, who does not recognize the finger of God. I am, therefore, tranquil: Russian opposition has failed, American opposition will fail. There will be American opposition; there will be, there is such already, in the very surroundings and cabinet of the President. We have just seen how it seeks to enervate his resolutions, to pledge him irrevocably to that wavering policy, more to be dreaded for him than the projects of assassination about which, right or wrong, so much noise has been made. Nevertheless, this evil has its bounds marked out in advance; he whom God guards is well guarded. If you wish to know what the Presidency of Mr. Lincoln will be in the end, see in what manner and under what auspices it was inaugurated; listen to the words that fell from the lips of the new President as he quitted his native town: "The task that devolves upon me is greater, perhaps, than that which has devolved on any other man since the days of Washington. I hope that you, my friends, will all pray that I may receive that assistance from on high, without which I cannot succeed, but with which success is certain." "Yes, yes; we will pray for you!" Such was the response of the inhabitants of Springfield, who, weeping, and with uncovered heads, witnessed the departure of their fellow-citizen. What a *debut* for a government! Have there been many inaugurations here below of such thrilling solemnity? Do uniforms and plumes, the roar of cannon, triumphal arches, and vague appeals to Providence, equal these simple words: "Pray for me!" "We will pray for you"! Ah! courage, Lincoln! the friends of freedom and of America are with you. Courage! you hold in your hands the destinies of a great principle and a great people. Courage! You have to resist your friends and to face your foes; it is the fate of all who seek to do good on earth. Courage! You will have need of it to-morrow, in a year, to the end; you will have need of it in peace and in war; you will have need of it to avert the compromise in peace or war of that noble progress which it is your charge to accomplish, more than in conquests of slavery. Courage! your rôle, as you have said, may be inferior to no other, not even to that of Washington: to raise up the United States will not be less glorious than to have founded them.

It is doubtless from a distance that we express these sympathies, but there are things which are judged better from a distance than near at hand.

Europe is well situated to estimate the present crisis. The opinion of France, especially, should have some weight with the United States: independently of our old alliances, we are, of all nations, perhaps, the most interested in the success of the Confederation. They are friendly voices which, here and elsewhere, in our reviews and our journals, bear to it the cordial expression of our wishes. In wishing the final triumph of the North, we wish the salvation of the North and South, their common greatness and their lasting prosperity.

But the South disquiets us; we cannot disguise it. It is in bad hands. A sort of terror reigns there; important but moderate men are forced to bow the head, or to feel that it will be necessary to do so ere long. The planters must see already that, in seeking to put away what they call the yoke of the North, they are preparing for themselves other masters. Business is suspended, money for cultivation is lacking, credit is everywhere refused, the ensuing harvest is mortgaged, the loans which it is sought to issue find no takers outside the extreme South. The resources of revolution remain, and they will be used unsparingly.

What a position! Under the Constitution voted scarcely a month ago, we already hear the deep rumbling of the quarrels of classes, of the planters and the poor whites, of the aristocracy and the numerical majority, of the prudent adversaries of the slave trade and its headstrong partisans, of the statesmen who are tolerated for appearances and those who count on replacing them, of the present and the future.

People will some day see clearly, even in Charleston. The separation which was to establish the prosperity of the South by permitting it at last to live to its liking, to obey its genius, and to serve its interests, has hitherto resulted in little, save the singing of the *Marseillaise*, (*the Marseillaise of Slavery!*) and the striking down of the Federal colors before the flag of the pelican and the rattlesnake. A great many blue ribbons and Colt's revolvers are sold; and busts of Calhoun, the first theorist of secession, are carried about ostentatiously. Next, to present a good mien to the eyes of Europe, a Constitution is voted in haste, a government is formed, an army is decreed; but the revolutionary basis is remaining, and we perceive but too quickly how great disorder prevails in minds and things.

At the present hour, the democracy of the South is about to degenerate into demagogism and dictatorship. But the North presents quite a different spectacle. Mark what is passing there; pierce beneath appearances, beneath inevitable mistakes, beneath the no less inevitable wavering of a *debut* so well prepared for by the preceding Administration, and you will find the firm resolution of a people uprising. Who speaks of the end of the United States? This end seemed approaching but lately, in the hour of prosperity; then, honor was compromised, esteem for the country was lowered, institutions were becoming corrupted apace; the moment seemed approaching when the Confederation, tainted by slavery, could not but perish with it. Now, every thing has changed aspect; the friends of America should take confidence, for its greatness is inseparable, thank God! from the cause of justice.

Justice cannot do wrong; I like to recall this maxim when I consider the present state of America. In escaping a sudden and shameful death, it will not, assuredly, escape struggles and difficulties; in returning to life, it will encounter battle and danger longer than it imagines; life is composed of this. To live is a laborious vocation, and nations who wish to keep their place here below, who wish to act and not to sleep, must know that they will have their share of suffering. Perhaps it enters into the plans of God that the United States should endure for a time some diminution of their greatness ; let them be sure, notwithstanding, that their flag will be neither less respected nor less glorious, if it shall thus lose a few of its stars. Those which it loses will reappear on it some day, and how many others, meanwhile, will come to increase the Federal Constellation! With what acclamations will Europe salute the future progress of the United States, as soon as their progress shall have ceased to be that of slavery!

At present, the point in question is to liquidate a bad debt. The moment of liquidation is always painful; but when it is over, credit revives. So will it be in America. She has often boasted of the energetic sang-froid of her merchants; when ruined, they neither lament, nor are discouraged; there is a fortune to make again. In the same manner, putting things at the worst, supposing the present crisis to be comparable to ruin; there is a nation to make again, it will be re-made. "Gentlemen," said Mr. Seward lately, in concluding his great speech in Congress, "if this Union were shattered to-day by the spirit of faction, it would reconstruct itself to-morrow with the former majestic proportions."

A WORD OF PEACE

ON THE DIFFERENCES BETWEEN ENGLAND AND THE UNITED STATES.

BY COUNT AGÉNOR DE GASPARIN.

A WORD OF PEACE.

Between the meetings of Liverpool and the ovations of New York, is there not room for a word of peace? A word of peace, I know well, must be a word of impartiality. The speaker must resign himself to be treated as an American in England, and as an Englishman in America; but what does this matter if truth make its way, and if an obstacle the more be raised in the way of this horrible war, this war contrary to nature, which would begin by ensuring the triumph of the champions of negro slavery, and would end by exposing the cause of free institutions to more than one perilous hazard?

There is one fundamental rule to follow in questions arising out of the right of search: to distrust first impressions. These are always very vivid. An insult to the honor of the flag is always in question. Patriotic sensibilities, which I comprehend and which I respect, are always brought into play. It is impossible that these officers, these stranger sailors, who have given commands and exacted obedience, who have stopped the ship on its way, who have set foot on the sacred deck where floats the banner of the country, who have interrogated, who have searched, who have had recourse, perhaps, to graver measures—it is impossible that they should not have called forth many sentiments of anger and indignation. Even when practised with the most rigid formalities, even when confined within the limits of the strictest legality, the right of search cannot fail to produce a feeling of annoyance. The recent search of the *Jules et Marie*, the yards of which were carried away and the barricadings driven in, seems to me the faithful type of all visits of search on the high seas—every one of them brings damages in its train.

Notwithstanding, the right of search is disputed by no one, and will be exercised in time of war, until the moment when the American proposition, reproduced again the other day by General Scott, shall be welcomed by our Old World.

I have just written the name of General Scott, and I did so with a feeling of pleasure. Whoever has read his letter, must have said to himself with me, that there exists in the United States a class of intelligent and moderate men—patriots, who have given proof of their capacity and are capable of examining dispassionately the demands of the English Government. These men know how much the maintenance of friendly relations with England is worth in the present position of America. Whatever opinion they may form on the question of right growing out of the action of Captain Wilkes, they comprehend that no consideration can weigh in the balance against the danger of bringing about the recognition of the Southern Confederacy, the breaking of the blockade, war, in short, with a powerful and friendly nation, a sister nation, sprung from the same blood, speaking the same language, devoted to the same mission of civilization and liberty. No honorable sacrifice would cost them too dear in order to avert this fearful catastrophe.

Would that they could see with their own eyes, were it but for a moment, what is passing to-day in Europe! Their enemies triumph, and their friends are struck with consternation. We, who have always loved America, and who love her better now that she is suffering for a noble cause; we who have defended her, we who have never ceased to believe in her final success, despite mistakes and repulses, feel all our hopes threatened at once; the ground seems sinking beneath our feet. No, we cannot suppose that America, in recklessness of heart, will destroy with her own hands the fruit of so many efforts and sacrifices. This would not be patriotism, it would not be dignity, it would be an act of madness and suicide.

If the *Trent* has violated the rules of neutrality, it remains none the less certain that other rules have been violated by the *San Jacinto*. The duty of naval officers is limited to visiting ships and stopping them, if need be, to carry them before a prize court. They cannot exercise the office of judge. In substituting the arrest of individuals for the seizure of ships, and a military act for a judicial decree, Captain Wilkes has given ground for the well-founded protests of England, at the same time that he has left the way open, thank God! for measures of reparation to be adopted by the United States.

I know very well that there would have been no less indignation at Liverpool and London in case that the *Trent* had been stopped on her way and carried before American courts. Perhaps, indeed, the regular and correct procedure would have been more deeply wounding than that of which

England complains. We may be permitted to doubt with General Scott that "the injury would have been less, had it been greater." But this is not the practical question, the only one that now concerns us. The point is to get out of embarrassment; and the error committed by the commander of the *San Jacinto* furnishes a reasonable ground for consenting to the liberation of the prisoners.

Far from being a humiliation to the Government at Washington, this act of wisdom would be one of its brightest titles to glory. It would prove that it is not wanting in moral power, that men calumniate it in representing it as the slave of a bad democracy, incapable of resisting the clamor of the streets, and of accepting, for the safety of the country, an hour of unpopularity.

Let it believe us, its true friends, that in arresting Messrs. Mason and Slidell, it has done more for the cause of the South than Generals Beauregard or Price would have done by winning two great victories on the Potomac and in Missouri. Messrs. Mason and Slidell are a hundred times more dangerous under the bolts of Fort Warren than in the streets of Paris or London; what their diplomacy would not certainly have obtained for them in many months, Captain Wilkes has procured for them in an hour. See what rejoicing is taking place in the camps of the Southern partisans! They were beginning to despair; recognition, that only chance of the defenders of slavery, seemed farther off than ever; the recent successes of the Federal army announced the commencement of a great change in affairs. The war was carried from the suburbs of Washington to the heart of South Carolina itself; the only resources of consequence remaining, were those that might spring up during the winter from the discontent of our industrial centres. Yet behold, suddenly, the state of affairs transformed; recognition becomes possible, the blockade is threatened, the United States are in danger of being forced to turn from the South to face a more redoubtable foe!

Really, what has Mr. Jefferson Davis done for you, that you should render him such a service!

Let us now turn to England, and tell her also the truth.

So long as England shall not treat the affair of the *Trent* on its own merits and with coolness, so long as she shall give ear to those falsehoods invented by passion, which envenom questions of this sort, and exclude conciliatory measures and pacific hopes, she will labor actively to destroy all that she has gloriously built upon earth. It is impossible to imagine the consequences, fatal to every form of liberty, which such a policy would comprise within itself.

It was at first supposed that Captain Wilkes had acted by virtue of instructions, and that Mr. Lincoln's Government had expressly ordered him to seize the Southern Commissioners on board the English vessel. Now it is found that Captain Wilkes, returning from Africa, had no instructions of any sort. He acted, to use his expression, "at his own risk and peril" like a true Yankee.

It was next supposed that Mr. Lincoln's Government had conceived the ingenious project (such things are gravely printed and find men to believe them!) of seeking of itself a rupture with England. It was in need of new enemies! It hoped, by this means, to rally to itself its present adversaries! It was about to give over combating them, and to seek compensation through the conquest of Canada! I have followed the progress of events in America as attentively as any one, I have read the American newspapers, I have received letters, I have studied documents, among others the famous circular of Mr. Seward; I have seen there more than one sign of discontent with the unsympathizing attitude of England; I have also seen there the symptoms of the somewhat natural fear which the intervention of Europe in Mexico excites in men attached to the Monroe doctrine; but as to these incredible plans, I have never discovered the slightest trace of them. I add, that a marked return towards friendly relations with England will be manifested the moment that the latter shows herself more amicable towards America.

If there is any quality for which credit cannot be refused to the Government of Mr. Lincoln, it is precisely that of moderation and good sense. He has not taken very high ground—he has abstained, far too much, in my opinion, from laying down those principles, from uttering those words which create sympathies, and make the conscience of the human race vibrate in unison. Say that he is a little prosaic, a little of the earth, earthy; do not say that he blusters, and that the best thing that England can do is to attack him without waiting to be first attacked.

In order to support, right or wrong, a fable which has found but too ready belief, another story was invented: the Government of Mr. Lincoln was at the end of its strength; despairing henceforth of conquering the South, it wished at any price to procure a diversion. Those who hold such language have doubtless never heard either of the Beaufort expedition, or of the evacuation of Missouri by the Confederate troops, or of the victory recently gained in Kentucky. They do not know that the United States have accomplished the prodigy of putting half a million of men under arms, that acts of insubordination have nearly ceased, that volunteers for three years have everywhere replaced the three months' volunteers. They do not know that the finances of the country are prosperous, and that Mr. Chase, the Secretary of the Treasury, has just negotiated, under favorable conditions, the last part of his loan. I recommend them to read the last letters of Mr. Russell, the correspondent of the *Times;* they will see there what an impartial witness thought lately of the respective chances of the North and South.

Yes, before the intervention of the *San Jacinto*, —that involuntary ally of the South, to whom the inhabitants of Charleston themselves ought to vote swords of honor—before the *San Jacinto*, the situation of the United States presented the most favorable aspect. Since that time, I admit, it has changed. Let us see now whether English indignation has not given to the act of Captain Wilkes greatly exaggerated proportions.

English indignation has omitted one side of the affair, I mean the conduct of the packet *Trent*. If, by chance, it should have violated the principles of neutrality, this question would wear quite a different aspect. This, doubtless, would not prevent the demand for reparation from being well founded; it would prevent the negotiations relating to it from assuming an air of harshness, which would suffice to render their success doubtful. Let us therefore examine the conduct of the *Trent*.

Some have thought to justify it, by observing that the vessel was going from America. What does this matter? Neutrals are bound to act as neutrals when they are going from a place as well as when they are coming towards it. They might as easily take sides with one of the belligerents by carrying despatches, for instance, designed to secure to it aid, as by bringing it other despatches announcing that this aid was forthcoming.

Others have based their arguments on the fact that the *Trent* had quitted a neutral port to repair to a neutral port. Again, a distinction which proclamations of neutrality have never admitted, and which no jurisprudence has endorsed to my knowledge. What does plain good sense tell us, in fact? That your departure from a neutral port and your destination to a neutral port do not hinder you in any way from serving the belligerent whose despatches you have received, especially if these despatches are on the way to solicit from a neutral country an alliance or supplies of munitions of war.

The rights of neutrals demand to be preserved, in my opinion, and France is interested in it more than any other nation. But these rights, let us not fear to acknowledge, have for their fundamental condition, a *real* neutrality. Now, you take it upon yourself, knowingly and willingly, to carry despatches destined for a country to which it is a notorious fact that one of the belligerents is looking for its only serious chances of success. These despatches are drawn up, it may be, in this wise: "Let vessels loaded with arms and ammunition leave Southampton or Liverpool as quickly as possible and come to Charleston, where the cruisers are now few in number; let expeditions be combined in such a manner as to force the blockade; we are in need of their arrival in order to push our army forward." Or else the despatches read: "Buy up the newspapers and work on public opinion in the manufacturing districts. Let maritime powers know that we will consent, if necessary, to cessions of territory or protectorates; that, in any case, we will grant them exceptional advantages if they protest against the blockade, if they disquiet our enemy, if they seek a quarrel with him and draw off his attention to fix it on an eventual struggle with Europe. At the first step of this kind, we will attempt an offensive movement. The least menace against the blockade is worth as much to us as the despatch of an army." Is it not to mock at people, in the face of so new a position, of a war in which one of the parties, though he does not fail to boast of his strength and his resources, counts in fact, before every thing, upon European support, to propound fine theories in accordance with which the transportation of despatches sent from a neutral port and destined for a neutral country, would not be contrary to neutrality, *because these despatches could not increase the military advantages of either of the belligerents?*

It has been sought to assimilate mail packets to vessels of war, and consequently to except them from the exercise of the right of search. The pretence is so ill-founded that it falls to the ground upon examination. Who does not feel that the presence of a lieutenant of the royal navy or the color of a uniform is not sufficient to constitute a vessel of war or a transport?

It is asked whether other packets, which have carried ministers sent by the United States to Europe, have not also infringed the rules of neutrality? It is possible, but this does not concern us. Supposing that the mission of these ministers in Europe, where they are regularly accredited like their predecessors to the different governments, and where they have no support, no new act, no violation of the blockade to demand, may be assimilated to the mission of the Southern delegates; supposing that their letters of credit bear some analogy to the despatches intrusted to Messrs. Mason and Slidell, it belonged in any case to the Southern cruisers to stop and search the packets in which they had taken passage. The powerlessness of one of the belligerents could not impose on the other the duty of abstaining in like manner.

Resting next on the diplomatic quality of the Southern envoys, it has been attempted to insinuate that their mission was purely a civil one. Not only did the diplomatic character not exist, since it had had no recognition, but the Southern Commissioners were expressly charged with procuring to the armies of slavery the most essential assistance which they could receive in view of military success and strategy. Their success, by ensuring the breaking of the blockade, would alone have been worth more to them than the winning of several battles. I say nothing, moreover, of the shipments of arms and ammunition which they would have doubtless organized in Europe.

Can it be that mail packets have the singular privilege of facilitating such operations without failing in the duties of neutrality? If this be true, it is worth while to have it understood, and so long as it is not understood, we must make some allowance for belligerents who do not consider it self-evident. It is clear that when the exercise of the right of search was defined by precedents and treaties, mail packets did not exist. Perhaps it would be well to lay down special regulations concerning them. This agreement might be profitably negotiated at present between the United States and the maritime powers of Europe. Why should not the conflict which occupies our attention, instead of ending in war, result in a useful negotiation? I have no doubt that the noble overtures, the initiative of which has just been taken by

General Scott, would be approved by Mr. Lincoln. To enlarge the scope of the present question, by causing an international progress, an emancipation of the commerce of the world to grow out of it, would be somewhat better, it seems to me, than to cut each other's throats and to ensure the triumph in the middle of the nineteenth century of the most shameful revolt that has ever broken out on earth—a revolt in favor of slavery. England and America, these two great countries, are worthy of giving to the world the spectacle of a generous and fruitful mutual understanding in which a deplorable disagreement shall be swallowed up, as it were, and disappear. Who does not see that, combined with the promulgation of a more liberal regulation of the right of search, the satisfaction demanded of the United States would assume a new character, and would have many more chances of being accorded?

It is the less difficult for the English to take this ground, since the act of the *San Jacinto*, in which the design of offending England in particular might at first have been suspected, appears to-day under a very different aspect. In proportion as we learn all the exploits of this terrible vessel, its impartiality becomes less dubious. French,

Danish, and other vessels were visited by it within a few days; it is certain that if the French instead of the English mail packet had been carrying the commissioners and their papers, the former would have been boarded by Captain Wilkes.

His mode of procedure was rough, and on this point apologies ought to be made. Not indeed that England, who has just sustained in Prussia the famous MacDonald negotiation, is in a very good position to show herself difficult in points of courtesy; nevertheless, the errors of Great Britain in Germany do not excuse those of the United States on the ocean. It appears that Captain Wilkes fired shot to enforce his first order to stop. The remainder was in keeping. Nevertheless, to give every one his due, it is just to remember that he offered to take on board the families of the commissioners and to give them his best cabins. It is just also to add that, after the arrest, the intercourse between the officers of the *San Jacinto* and the prisoners never ceased to be full of decorum and courtesy.

Let us now approach more closely the question of right. It was well in the first place to rid ourselves of secondary questions which hinder us from seeing it, and above all from seeing it as it is.

They seem to have been afraid in England to look this question of right boldly in the face. There is no subterfuge that they have not tried in order to avoid its serious investigation.

Have they not gone so far as to object to the United States that, considering the Southen States as rebellious and refusing them the quality of belligerents, they could not exercise the right of search, which is reserved to belligerents? From this point of view they add, Messrs. Mason and Slidell would simply be rebels taking refuge under the English flag; and what country would consent to give up political refugees? The answer is simple: no country more than England has recognized, in this instance, the quality of belligerents which her partisans are seeking to contest in her name. Moreover, the Southern blockade is admitted by her and by the other powers; now, blockade is as impossible as right of search apart from a state of war.

Another subterfuge: the United States have always opposed the right of search—it ill becomes them to exercise it. England has always exercised the right of search; it ill becomes her to oppose it. Let us be honest; rights of this kind are always odious to those who submit to them and always dear to those who profit by them. Alas! this is not the only instance in which a change in our position works a change in our mode of viewing things. Let us take the human heart as it is, and not demand under penalty of war, that the Americans, in the midst of one of the most terrible social crises (and also of the most glorious) of which history makes mention, should hesitate to seize a weapon which was formerly used against them and which they feel the need of using in return. In neglecting to seize it, they would fail perhaps in their duty to themselves and to the noble cause of which they are the representatives.

There is finally a last and more simple manner of avoiding an embarrassing examination: "What is the use of examining precedents?" we hear on every side, "This is not a matter for legal advisers." It appears to me, however, that it is something of the kind, since Great Britain has begun by interrogating the lawyers of the Crown, and since she has made peace or war depend on the decision which they might render. It would be too convenient, truly, to take exception to precedents made by one's self, and to say to those who act as he has not ceased to do: "I permit no one to imitate me; what I practised in times past, I authorize no one to practise to-day. I have not apprised you of this, but you ought to have divined it, and for not having divined it, you shall have war."

Precedents keep then their full value. What are they?

The enemies of America have cited one which has nothing to do here; the letter written by King Louis Philippe to Queen Victoria to express his regret that a pilot under the protection of the British flag had been carried away by the expedition bound to Mexico. A very different thing is an abduction of this kind, having nothing in common with the right of search or the maintenance of neutrality, and the capture of the Southern Commissioners.

It is in the familiar history of the right of search that precedents must be sought, and they abound there.

In quoting some of them, I impose on myself a double law: first, I will not confound acts of violence with precedents, and from the abuse which the English made in times past of their maritime preponderance, I will not conclude that every one is at liberty to do to-day as they have done; secondly, among the grave and weighty authors who have made a special study of these questions in the quiet of their retirement, I will confine myself to consulting none but English authorities. Doubtless, they will not think of challenging these in England.

Chancellor Kent writes: "If, on making the search, it be discovered that the vessel is employed in contraband trade, that it transports the enemy's property, troops, or *despatches*, it may be rightfully seized and carried for adjudication before a prize court."

Mr. Phillimore, an English author and an authority on these questions, and one of the judges in the Admiralty, expresses himself thus: "The carrying of official despatches written by official personages on the public affairs of one of the belligerents, *impresses a hostile character on those bearing them.*"

Sir William Scott is no less precise: "The transportation of two or three shiploads of ammunition is necessarily a limited assistance; *but, by despatches, the whole plan of the campaign may be transmitted in such a manner as to destroy all the plans of the other belligerent in that part of the world.*" And he dwells at length on this idea, insisting on the incompatibility which exists between veritable neutrality and the bearing of despatches, "which is an act of the most prejudicial and hostile nature."

Let us also cite Mr. Jenkinson, afterwards Lord Liverpool. He establishes in clear terms the fundamental principle of the matter by putting this question, which plain good sense must answer: "Can it be lawful for you to extend this right (that of the free navigation of neutral vessels) in such a way as to injure me and to serve my enemy?"

Observe that the Queen, in her proclamation of neutrality, has been careful not to omit the interdiction of the transport of despatches. She therein declares that those who transport "officers, soldiers, *despatches*, arms, ammunition, or any other article considered by law and modern usage as contraband of war, for either of the contenders, will do it at his own risk and peril, and will incur the high displeasure of her Majesty."

Nothing can be more explicit, more consistent, and at the same time more reasonable than these declarations. Sir William Scott is right in saying, that, in undertaking to carry despatches, persons cease to be neutrals and become enemies; this is evident, above all, in the present conflict. As the serious chances of success of the South are all in Europe, as it would not have revolted had it not counted on Europe, as it would lay down its arms to-morrow if it were proved to it that never, for cotton or any thing else, would Europe come to its aid, it follows, thenceforth, that the despatches forwarded from the South to Europe greatly surpass in military importance the sending of soldiers or supplies.

This being so, what ought the commander of the packet *Trent* to have done? I do not impugn his intentions, he may have acted very innocently; but if this excuse of ignorance of the rules of the law be valid for him, I think that it should also be so for Captain Wilkes, and that there would be little justice in treating with extreme rigor a first offence which evidently has taken every one by surprise, and has found nowhere a very complete understanding of the conditions of the right of search.

The commander of the *Trent* saw men come to him, whose quality as Southern Commissioners challenged his attention. He knew what anxiety and trouble were pervading the North concerning their mission and despatches, the contents of which excited grave suspicions; there had even been talk, exaggerated, doubtless, of a proposition of a protectorate and other offers, designed to gain at any price the support of one or more maritime powers. The enthusiastic welcome which the people of Havana, enemies of the United States, and ardent friends of slavery, had just given to Messrs. Mason and Slidell, permits no doubt of the especial gravity of the hostile mandate with which they were charged. Then or never was the occasion to say that messengers and messages of this nature must travel under their own flag, and that neutrals were bound not to facilitate their mission in any manner. In circumstances so grave, and with such a responsibility, commanders of packets could not take refuge behind their innocence, or argue that the consul of the United States had not taken pains to forewarn them. I should like to know what reception a neutral would find in England, who should take it into his head to say to her: "I thought myself at liberty to carry hostile despatches and those bearing them, because the English consul did not come to bind me to do nothing of the sort."

Is it true, as has been maintained, that the fault was divided, the message having been carried by one packet and the messengers by another? This appears doubtful, and matters little, moreover, in the eyes of impartial judges. The fact is, that voluminous papers were seized on the *Trent*, at the same time with the rebel commissioners.

Now, and to have done with the question of right, shall I say a few words of what it is permissible to call the hackneyed rhetoric and declamation of the subject?

Men have talked, of course, of an insult to the flag; they have called to mind that the deck of an English vessel is the same as the soil of the country; they have invoked the rights of British hospitality, and demanded whether she could consent to see her guests taken from her by force. So many phrases for effect, which unhappily never fail to arouse implacable passions! But what is there behind these phrases?

The flag is not insulted when the search is exercised in conformity with the law of nations. It is in vain that the deck of an English merchant vessel is the soil of the country; a belligerent is authorized to seize it, if it is carrying men employed in behalf of the enemy; officers, for example. The rights of hospitality are bounded by the duties of neutrality, and the vessel which would claim to protect its guests at any price, when its guests serve the war, would simply be guilty of a culpable action.

In brief, there are wrongs on both sides, and if ever difference admitted of discussion, interpretation, if necessary, arbitration even, it is certainly this. Be sure, therefore, that Europe, attentive to all that is passing, and desirous of averting war, will find it inexplicable if the question be put in insulting terms, of a nature to render hostilities almost inevitable.

If, in fine, Captain Wilkes had seized the vessel instead of seizing the Commissioners, and if the vessel had been duly condemned by an American court, the proceeding would have been irreproachably regular. This being so, by the acknowledgment of the English themselves, who will be willing to admit that any will be found bold enough to cause an irretrievably fatal rupture to grow out of a quarrel of this kind, concerning the mode of procedure. England has consulted her legal advisers; America will consult hers also. Do disputes in which the national honor is involved admit of consultations of this sort? Are lawyers or judges ever asked whether the country is insulted or attacked when it really is so?

Let England assure herself that the first condition of the demand for reparation is, that she shall make the reparation *possible.* Time is needed. Patience is needed—patience which will not pause before the first difficulty, and take as final the first refusal. Courtesy is needed—courtesy, which, in the stronger, agrees so well with dignity, and avoids rendering the form of satisfaction unnecessarily wounding and consequently almost inadmissible. It is clear that if she contents herself with signifying to Washington an absolute demand, if she gives a single week, if she exacts (let us foresee the impossible) not only the setting at liberty of the Commissioners themselves, but their transportation on an American vessel charged to trail its repentant flag across the seas, if she accepts no more easy mode, if she hearkens to no mediation, it is clear that Mr. Lincoln will need superhuman courage to grant what she thus demands.

This superhuman courage I wish for him, I ask of him; in displaying it, he will have deserved much of America and of humanity. But I hope little for such marvels, nor do I believe that it is fitting to exact miracles in serious affairs.

The English were full of condescension and generosity towards America while she was strong. If they should be so unfortunate as no longer to have condescension and generosity towards America, when she is weak, they would warrant suppositions much more fatal to their honor than is the grave error (yet easily reparable with the good will of both parties) just committed by Captain Wilkes.

I have the right to hold this language to them, for I am of the number of those who love England and have proved it. In my first parliamentary speech, which was on occasion of this very right of search, I exposed myself to much animosity in defending her. Later, in the Pritchard affair, I did not draw back. Even from the depths of my retreat, it has rarely happened to me to take up my pen without rendering homage to a country and government which are not popular among us. I have reason, therefore, to hope that my words will have some weight. Nothing is more antipathetic to me than a coarse and ignorant anglophobia.

But it is important for England to know all the phases of the debate in which she has entered. It has a European phase. This is not a discussion between two powers; a third, the first of all, public opinion, must also have its say. It wishes peace, and will not let it be sacrificed for an error easily repaired and voluntarily exaggerated. Public opinion strongly repudiates the cause of the South, which is that of slavery; (the speeches of Mr. Stephens, Vice-President of the Southern Confederacy, give proof of this.) At the announcement of the heinous fact that England recognizes the Confederacy expressly founded to maintain, glorify, and extend slavery, public opinion, believe me, would give vent to an outburst of wrath which would cast the indignation meetings of Liverpool wholly in the shade.

England has maintained her neutrality in the New World for the year past, and she deserves well for this, for angry instincts dictated to her another policy. However, if she has been neutral, she has not been sympathizing. This vast social revolution, which began with the election of Mr. Lincoln, which had inscribed on its banner, "No extension of slavery," and which thus entered in the way leading one day to emancipation; this generous revolution which deserved to be encouraged, has met with little in England but distrust and hostility. Upon other points, while preserving her neutrality, England knows very well how to give her moral support to causes which she loves—the support of journals, of parliamentary speeches, and of public meetings. Here, there is nothing of the sort. I know not what fatal misunderstanding has kept down the generous sentiments which should have made themselves felt. From the beginning, the principal English journals, especially those reputed to express the views of Lord Palmerston, have not ceased to proclaim openly that the South was right in seceding, that the separation was without remedy, that it was just and in conformity with the wishes of England. Again and again has the recognition of the South been presented as an act to be expected and for which we must be prepared.

From all this, if care be not taken, the inference will be drawn that, in the excessive eagerness with which the affair of the *Trent* has been seized upon, in the peremptory terms of the demand for redress, in the form adopted in order to render the reparation difficult, may be seen the intention of reaching the end which England proposes; of effecting the recognition, breaking the blockade, obtaining cotton, and substituting a parcelled-out America for the too powerful Republic of the United States.

Liverpool has, this time, given the signal, Lancashire urges on the rupture; behind the national honor, there may be something else. Take care! if this must not be thought, it must not be true.

And it will be true if you declare the question closed at the very moment when it begins to attract public attention; if you exact a reparation without admitting an explanation; if, in short, you reject in advance all idea of negotiation, mediation, or arbitration.

War, instead of negotiation, mediation, or arbitration; war, at the first word, for a question which has been submitted to legal advisers, and which offers facilities assuredly for several equally sincere intepretations; *war at any price* does not belong to our times.

What I say here, others will make it their business to say on the other side of the channel; there have been, there will be, liberal and Christian voices there, who will not fear to protest against the incitements of passion. We have heard little yet except the bells of the manufactories; other sounds will soon make themselves heard; the great party which, in abolishing slavery and combating the slave trade, has won the chief title of honor in England—this great party, I think, is not dead. It is time for it to give signs of life.

As to America, its friends are awaiting its final resolutions with an anxiety which I scarcely dare depict. Never was graver question placed before a government. The whole future is contained in it. If she be sufficiently mistress of herself to grant what is asked and to admit a reparation, even though it be excessive, of the fault evidently committed in her name, she will have the approbation and esteem of all true hearts. Her ship—the ship which brings back the Commissioners—will be welcomed with acclamations to our shores, and it will be plainly seen that the United States in yielding much is neither weakened nor humiliated.

Ah! the affair would be so easily arranged, if both sides desired it! On both sides are men so worthy to effect a reconciliation for the glory of our times and the happiness of humanity! On both sides are nations so well fitted to understand and to love each other! Must we despair then of the progress of the spirit of peace? Must we look with our own eyes upon English vessels employed in ensuring the success of the champions of slavery? Must we veil our head with our mantle?

A. DE GASPARIN.

VALLEYRES, (SWITZERLAND,)
December 5, 1861.

P. S.—I wish to add here a single observation:

I have not pretended to exhaust, in this rapid study, the decisions which might be borrowed from English authors, and which would be of a kind to be appealed to by America. Sir William Scott, for example, (see C. Robinson, p. 467,) says in express terms: "*You may stop the ambassador of your enemy.*" I have been careful not to draw the conclusion from this, on my part, that Captain Wilkes was right in acting as he did; I simply infer from it that the case is by no means a hanging one, and that in stopping the Commissioners and their papers without stopping the ship and turning her from her course, he yielded perhaps (let us be just to all) to the desire of not exposing the packet and passengers to serious inconveniences. Let us say that he was unfortunate, since his courtesy on this point seems to have become the blackest of his misdeeds. In truth, to see in the affair of the *Trent*, all that England has seen in it, it is necessary to commence by supposing that the United States, which have already a sufficiently heavy task on their hands, it seems to me, have been tempted, besides, to procure a quarrel with Great Britain. Hypotheses of this kind will be welcomed only by those who feel themselves unconquerably impelled to praise the messages of Mr. Jefferson Davis, and to stretch their hand decidedly to the brave South, which has so much to complain of, and which is defending so just a cause! *

* This article, with the exception of a few changes and additions, was inserted in the *Journal des Débats*, December 11, 12, and 13.

www.ingramcontent.com/pod-product-compliance
Lightning Source LLC
LaVergne TN
LVHW020241110826
845151LV00003B/992

9781425529871